DON'T STOP BELIEVING!

D1452548

by
Reggie Vinson
"Rockin' Reggie Vincent"

Harrison House
Tulsa, Oklahoma

Don't Stop Believing
ISBN 1-57794-273-6
Copyright © 2000 by Reggie Vinson

Published by Harrison House, Inc.
P. O. Box 35035
Tulsa, Oklahoma 74153

DEDICATION

When I first stepped out in faith to do God's work I was invited to be a guest on TBN with Paul and Jan Crouch. The other guests on that show were Buddy and Pat Harrison. After the show, Buddy said, "Reggie, you need to write a book." I said, "Someday, I will."

Through the years, Buddy asked me more than once, "Reggie, when are you going to write that book?" I would always tell him, "Someday, I will."

So, Buddy, this is for you, in memory of our friendship.

I also want to thank my adopted dad, Lee Eller, and my spiritual parents, Dr. Kenneth E. Hagin Sr. and Mrs. Oretha Hagin, for their love and support during all the years of our friendship.

I want to thank my wife, Sadie, our children and my son-in-law, Russ Baker, for their prayers and encouragement during the writing of this manuscript. And to Mom, Pop and Sissy: I love you.

Thanks to my secretary, Regina Brooks, for her prayers, her candid comments and her straightforward suggestions.

Special thanks to three men who gave me their pulpits for a Sunday morning: Dr. Jerry Landry, Dr. Lester Sumrall and Pastor John Osteen. Even though they are no longer here in the flesh, they will always have a special place in my heart.

To all my friends and fellow pastors and ministers mentioned in this book, and all those who have gone before us, thank you for your help.

And always, thank You, Jesus.

CONTENTS

FOREWORD

The best dreams are the ones that don't come with any maps or directions, let alone with any promises or guarantees.

They're the ones that seem so far away, so hard to reach that lots of people say you just can't do it.

They say you should be more practical, more realistic, and after a while, you almost start believing them—but not quite, because deep down in your heart, you believe in yourself.

INTRODUCTION

Sure, I've met frustration, and I don't like him. I know discouragement, despair and all those other downers. But I guess I always knew that sooner or later something good was bound to happen to me.

Some people grow old without ever being able to overcome their inner conflicts. No matter what they actually accomplish, they always question their own worth. They live with their fears of failure and rejection, until their fears become realities.

No matter what they achieve, it's never enough. They long for a solution to uncertainty, some higher purpose, something to make them realize who they are and give them confidence.

I hope the following story will explain why I had the courage to write about my life. Not intended to be a report on my life and times, it is part autobiography and part handbook for dreamers. I believe it will be an encouragement to everyone—not just dirty laundry. This was not easy, and it was not meant to offend or belittle anyone: It's just the truth.

GROWING UP IS SO HARD TO DO!

I've always been a dreamer. Always. I suppose it's because my mother fed me faith with my baby food. She always told me, "Nothing is impossible to those who believe."

Faith came easy for her: faith to believe your dreams can come true, faith to believe in a God who answers prayers and wants the best for His children.

I've known since I was a little boy that if you want something enough to work hard for it and you never let the dream die, you stand a good chance of succeeding.

Of course, the world will tell you differently. There is always somebody out there waiting to tell you that you'll never make it, you'll never be a success, you can't get there from here, you've made too many wrong turns already, it's impossible. But Mom always told me that I would get what I asked for—one way or another—so I ask for a lot.

By the way, my name is Reggie Vinson.

Anyone who's ever been to a shoutin', singin' Pentecostal gathering knows about the roots of rock and roll. It was conceived in the countryside, born in the blues and weaned in the churches. Jimi Hendrix was raised a Baptist. Sam Cooke began as a gospel singer. So did Marvin Gaye, Aretha Franklin, B.B. King and Little Richard. But as rock

and roll found the roadhouses and juke joints, the churches cast it out as the "devil's music."

Playing rock and roll was what I wanted to do more than anything else, but I didn't talk a lot about it in front of my parents, because they were mostly into gospel music. In the church we attended, rock and roll was considered straight from the pits of hell. Other than my love for rock and roll, I was a good son. I was even baptized one time on a trip down to Tennessee in one of those creek baptisms so many Southern churches have. Even though I was afraid of the water, I went when the preacher called to me.

But being a good son and being baptized didn't change my heart or make everything right between God and me. I didn't know it, but I was missing something: a personal relationship with Him through His Son.

My mom, Lillie, was an old-time, Church of God of Prophecy, guitar-pickin' gospel singer. My father, Virgil,

Creek Baptism

was a dirt farmer from down in Putnam County, Tennessee. Both came from large and poor, never-had-much, barely-livin'-off-the-land families from the hills. They were married young, and I was their second child, born in Cookeville, Tennessee. My sister, Athylene, was four years older. I called her Sissy.

When I was still a child, about seven or eight, we moved to Detroit so my dad could work in a Ford assembly plant. But much of our free time centered on the church and gospel music. My grandfather had been a preacher in the hills of Tennessee and Kentucky. He was tall, like me, and wore a black jacket and black pants, and a tall black hat like I've seen Abraham Lincoln wear in portraits. Because of him, evangelists and preachers used to stay at our home when they came to hold services in town.

My dad was gentle and willing to listen to my childhood dreams. We spent a lot of time together doing chores and talking. Well, I did most of the talking.

But he was also the disciplinarian in our family and could be very strict. One day, I got into trouble when I came home so late after playing with my friends that I missed going to church. My family had gone without me, and I just knew I was in trouble. When Dad got home, he laid on the spanking. After he wiped away my tears, he kissed me, said, "I love you," and sent me to bed.

It's true about a parent hurting more than a child when the parent has to punish his own flesh-and-blood. But when you're a child you don't know that. I'd have none of his "I love you." I was so mad that I marched into my room and yelled, "God, I wish he was dead!"

That night—it was a Wednesday, I'll never forget—Mama woke me up, and in the darkness I heard her say, "Dad is real sick. I'm taking him to the hospital." I ran into his bedroom and felt his forehead. He was so still. I started crying. I knew he was dead—I just knew it.

I threw my arms around him and told him how sorry I was for saying those words. I cried, "God, You can't do this! I didn't mean it!"

A neighbor came over to stay with Sissy and me while Mom went with Dad in the ambulance. As the flashing lights disappeared, I fled into my room, fell on my knees and prayed, as most twelve-year-olds would: "God, please don't take my daddy, please! I was only kidding—what I said. I'll even give up my toys if You won't take him." It was guilt I felt then—and for a long time after.

About an hour or so later, Mom came home. Her face told me before I even heard her words. Dad had a stroke. He never awakened. She put her arms around Sissy and me. "Daddy's gone to be with Jesus."

How could this be? I wanted to know.

After the funeral in Detroit, his body was flown to Tennessee. The car trip down there seemed endless. Then my daddy was buried. It's the hardest thing in the world for a child to watch his parent's body lowered into the ground, to see the dirt shoveled over the casket, to know that it's all over. It's hard because your future is still ahead of you but now you don't know what that'll bring. What does a child do without his father?

A preacher came by. "Son," he told me, "God decided to take your daddy home because He needed him in heaven. So you be big now, and accept this."

When we got back to Detroit, I asked, "Mom, how are we gonna make it now?" I believed God had deserted me, failed to answer my prayers at the direst moment. *Why? Why did He let my daddy die?* I asked myself. I was responsible for his death, or so I thought. Then I had asked for help—and had gotten nothing. So, in my anger, I turned my back on Him. I gave up on God, on the church and even on music. My dream had died with my daddy!

But even though I turned my back on God, He never turned His back on me. Though it would be years before I looked for Him and discovered that He had not taken my daddy from me, He was always ready to rekindle our relationship. Even my love for music was soon to revive.

I remember being in grade school in Detroit and hearing someone singing on a friend's radio during recess. The song was "That's All Right Mama." I asked who it was that was singing. "Elvis!" And what's that music? "Rock and roll!"

When the last bell rang, I ran home just as fast as I could. There was my mom in the kitchen, singing and playing her old Sears Roebuck Silvertone guitar. In the hills of Tennessee, where she came from, everybody played some kind of an instrument, even if it was just a washboard or a jug. Most sang too. I went over and sat down next to her. I watched her play, more interested than I'd ever been before.

"Can you teach me the guitar? Please, Mom, please."

"Reggie, what do you want to play guitar for anyway?"

"Because music makes me happy. And it makes other people happy too."

"Okay, I'll teach you." The first song she showed me was a religious one—"What A Friend We Have In Jesus." This was not rock and roll.

"That's real nice, Mom, but how about something fast? Do you know any Elvis songs? Or how about that Ricky Nelson song he sings on television—'Hello, Mary Lou'?"

She played it for me. It wasn't particularly hard. There were only three chords—G, C and D. Before long I realized that most every song those days, fast or slow, had only those same three chords in them. I practiced them over and over again. I remember playing "That's All Right Mama" until my fingertips bled. But I felt no pain. I wanted to rock-away the world.

My sister, Sissy, was already in high school and was listening to Jimmy Reed, B.B. King and Chuck Berry. When I heard Bo Diddley, I learned his guitar shuffles, and I bought his records and studied them.

The better I got, the bigger show-off I became. I'd be the life of the party whenever my relatives or my parents' friends would gather at the house. Mom, Sis and I would play and sing, but I would always be the star—or at least that's what I thought.

Mom had to find work to support us now, and wanting to help, I took an early morning job standing on a corner selling newspapers. But it didn't last long. I was never much for regular jobs.

When Mom started dating Charlie Guffey, I was happy—and even happier when they mentioned marriage. That would mean I'd have a daddy again. Once they did marry, though, I realized that Charlie was more my mom's husband than my father. He was a good man, but he could never fill the empty space left by the loss of my father. Now I felt, instead of gaining a father, I was losing my mother too. My grandfather had died just before my daddy, and now my grandmother on my mama's side died too. Then Sissy married. It seemed my whole family was slipping away from me.

I'd been a fairly good student at Edison Elementary in Dearborn, but now when I moved on to the Annapolis Junior High near Detroit, I began to rebel—and there was no one to get me back on track. I guess I wanted someone to look up to, because most of my friends were older. I was six feet tall even at that age, so I fit in with the older crowd. I made friends with the toughest guy in junior high and took on his act—cocky, hateful, despising school—and my grades showed it.

Church? All I heard was "don't do this" and "don't do that." "You can't go to movies." "It's wrong to wear jewelry." "Stay away from girls." "Don't listen to this rock and roll." Well, I wanted to do all those things.

I was trying to be a "hip hood" and doing as much as I could to prove that I was a man—skipping school, drinking, taking drugs. I thumbed my nose at authority and found I could get away with it. No one was going to tell me what to do. Everything that I'd been taught was forbidden fruit now tasted so sweet.

We got our kicks by ditching class and walking down the street until we spotted a car with the ignition keys inside. We'd pile in and cruise around, looking for girls and booze, having a joyride until the car ran out of gas. Then we'd jump out and walk home, acting all carefree and innocent. Three times I was caught and arrested. But none of those times made an impression on me.

One day I ran away from home with a girl, who was more than willing, stealing a car and booze along the way. We were Bonnie and Clyde cruising down the highway, heading south.

Our getaway lasted 450 miles. It was two in the morning when the Illinois Highway Patrol pulled us over. They handcuffed us and took us to jail.

I was in with two seasoned criminals—one a robber, the other a wife beater—because they thought I was twenty-one. So did everyone else, apparently: In addition to the car theft charge, the girl's parents had charged me with statutory rape. Then, as soon as we crossed state lines, the FBI, who had been called in on the dragnet met us. My false bravado wore off when I found that I could be sentenced to the State Penitentiary for seven to fifteen years.

I sat in jail for seven days, waiting, marking off each day that passed on the prison wall with a spoon (I was never one lacking in dramatics). I'll never forget the black, black coffee or the plain, plain doughnuts we were fed every day. Finally, my mom came and proved my real age. I was released: out on probation.

But I had learned nothing from the experience. In fact, I became even more arrogant. I had been wanted by the FBI, and now that I was out of danger, I wore it as a badge of rebellion. I was Marlon Brando and James Dean. I was "the wild one," "the rebel without a cause."

Then, for the first time since my daddy had died, I picked up my guitar again. I don't know why. Maybe I just had the music in me. I began jamming with local groups, organizing bands. While at Lowry High School, I worked days at a grocery store so I could spend the nights in my first blues band, playing harmonica, singing Jimmy Reed songs. I was definitely cool—"big boss man."

But high school was clearly a drag for someone like me who thought he had better things to do than listen to a bunch of dried-out grownups talk about outdated ideas and dead people. So I quit.

I went to work at the Tulsa Oil Company painting gas stations, and I bought my first car—an old '53 Chevy. It cost me seventy-five dollars. It had bald tires and burned as much oil as gas—but they were *my* "wheels." The next year I graduated to a fastback Ford—like one right out of *American Graffiti* or *Happy Days*—with dice hanging from the rearview mirror and, hand painted on the side, "Lonely One."

James Dean once said that only three things motivated people: sex, love and money. Rock and roll encompassed all of them; and for most teenagers, rock and roll means power—the power to upset parents, the power to get sex, the power to gain self-esteem and, perhaps, fame.

When I was still seventeen, I carried false ID that said I was twenty-two. I moved in with the top stripper in Detroit. Her stage name was Rita Rogers. We'd met at a club where I was playing with my band, which was making the rounds of low-class dives and better-paying strip clubs. I was attracted to her, and she was attracted to me because I was a rock and roller.

One night after she finished working, we went to an after-hours party (anything after 2:00 A.M. was illegal) known as a 'blind pig,' which stayed open and often had gambling. There was a sleazy assortment of pushers, hookers and syndicate people. Two police detectives had invited us, but I was definitely shocked when I was introduced to a highly placed city official who had a hooker on each arm and was smoking a big cigar—just like in the movies.

I loved the sense of the underworld and the danger. That's part of the lure of rock and roll too: being on the edge. Taking drugs, dating strippers, leaping into the audience and smashing instruments are merely effects. The cause is the excitement, the rush you get from living on the precipice. It's something you can get hooked on as surely as heroin—and it's just as dangerous.

Reggie, Mom and Sissy

LIKE A ROLLING STONE

One day, my dream took me to a bus station. I was a tall, skinny kid with a guitar and a lot of guts. For show business, that wasn't going to be enough. I needed more. I needed to be more. I needed a stage name.

I was going to New York to see Bob Johnson, manager and producer of Bob Dylan. *"Bob." Johnson will like that. Now the last name....* Everybody was trying to latch on to the British invasion. *Invasion...England...London. Bob London. Not enough. Think big. Bob London and...Bob London and the Bobbies.* There was no Bob London, no Bobbies—but they were good rock and roll names. If I succeeded, I would be Bob London. I'd find the Bobbies somewhere. *If?* I was going to be as big as the Beatles!

I stepped from the bus and into a beautiful New York City morning. In a new place with a new name. There were a lot of people—all strangers in a strange city. But before I'd walked only a few blocks, I noticed four longhaired guys, and they saw me. I had long hair too, and in the sixties that meant we had something more in common—especially since I was carrying my guitar and amp.

"Hey, do you play in a band?" one of them asked.

"No, but I'm a songwriter and guitarist. Are you guys in a band?"

"Yeah, man, we're 'The Lovin' Spoonful.'"

I couldn't believe it. "Wow! I just heard you on the radio, and you guys are great! I'm Reg–, uh, Bob London."

They asked me to come down to the Village, where they were playing that night, and to bring my guitar.

"Yeah, I will. Where's the Village?"

"Just ask anyone. They'll know."

I told them "thanks" and turned to walk away. "Hey, what's your name?" I shouted to the one wearing glasses.

"John Sebastian."

I'm in New York for less than an hour, and already I'm meeting rock and roll stars. Now it's my turn!

I hurried down the hallway of the building, lugging my guitar, amp and suitcase to Johnson's office. At nine in the morning, it was already busy.

"Can I help you?" his secretary asked.

"Yes, I'm Bob London from Detroit. I rode a bus all night to get here, and I'd like to play a song for Bob Johnson."

She told me to wait. So I sat down, took my guitar from its case and plugged my amp into an outlet.

Immediately she said, "You can't do that!"

Just then Johnson walked in. "Hey, kid, you can't play electric guitar in here. This is a place of business."

"But..."

"You have an acoustic?"

"No."

"Get yourself one. Then I'll listen to you."

You know the nightmare every school kid has where you're in class and stand up to answer a question and suddenly realize you're stark naked? That's how I felt as everyone in the office watched me pack away my things and walk out. I couldn't leave fast enough; it seemed I was moving in slow motion.

On the street again, I was too numb to be depressed. The sky had darkened. It began to rain.

But no one stays in one place for long. One step leads to another, and before long you're down the street and around the corner. In my case, "around the corner" was a little pawnshop. Inside was an acoustic guitar. The broker said he'd loan it to me for $100. I only had $50. But I was willing to do whatever I had to. I traded him my suitcase, my guitar and my amp. He handed me the acoustic and $50.

I ran through the rain back up the street, trying to keep the precious guitar from getting wet. I rushed into Johnson's office gasping for air.

Again his secretary told me to take a seat, and I waited ...and waited...and waited. Finally, she told me Mr. Johnson was busy. *Dreams dashed, trip for nothing, failure.* "But his assistant will listen to your song." *I'm gonna be a star!*

I followed the young assistant into his office and nervously began to tune my guitar. Surprisingly, in walked Johnson, momentarily freed from his other commitments. "Okay, kid, let's hear what you got."

I played one song, and he seemed to like what he heard. He asked me to play another, so I did. I was getting really excited when he had asked me to play two more and hadn't thrown me out of the office yet.

I knew that the words that would bust open the gates of rock and roll heaven were on the tip of his tongue: *"Son, you are a talent the likes of which I haven't heard since I first met little Bobby Zimmerman from Hibbing, Minnesota. Let's get you a record contract and start making you famous."*

I was ready. I smiled. But he didn't say those magic words. Johnson just looked at me for a moment. "Okay, I've heard enough. What's your name?"

"Bob."

"Bob, I can tell you have the desire to be a star."

Here it comes.

"But...you're not ready yet." The verdict was in, and the defendant condemned. The hangman's noose was around my neck; I didn't move for fear it would tighten.

"Let me give you some advice," said Johnson as he showed me the way to the door. "Only the strong survive."

That was it. What a letdown! I had come to the Big Apple with dreams of gold records flashing in my mind, but the dreams had vanished and left me with a sick feeling inside.

Outside, the rain was coming down in torrents. I returned to the pawnshop and swapped the acoustic for my electric gear. I never did make it to the Village to jam with the Lovin' Spoonful. Instead, suitcase in hand, I boarded the bus and headed back to Detroit. That was the end of Bob London and the Bobbies.

MOTOR CITY

The Royal Playboys were already a well-known Detroit rock group when they saw me play in another band and asked me to join them. For a seventeen-year-old to join a band that already had a record contract was a big deal. Soon we produced "Bo," an instrumental Bo Diddley-style song that was a major regional hit. It became a top-ten song on CKLW, the top rock station for Detroit and Canada, located in Windsor, Canada.

On the same record label was another rising star—Chico Holiday, whose bass player, Harvey Brooks, had played on Bob Dylan's "Like a Rollin' Stone." We first met at a party thrown for local deejays and producers when the Royal Playboys began to get noticed.

The Royal Playboys were booked throughout Michigan and Ohio. Our first big concert was opening for Herman's Hermits. We also opened up for Sam the Sham and The Pharaohs ("Wooly, Boolly") and the Dave Clark Five at the Ohio State Fair.

When we heard Chuck Berry needed a band for a concert in Ohio and was paying $500, we were there. But as the opening act was playing, there was still no Chuck Berry. No one knew where he was or what to do if he never showed. Then up pulled this big Cadillac. Chuck

Berry. He was alone and obviously had been drinking. He jumped out, grabbed a beer, sucked it down and said, "Who's got my money, and where's my band? Okay, let's go play some rock and roll."

"But...Mr. Berry...what...?"

He kept on moving, and the band followed. As we ran on to the stage, I finally caught up with him. "Mr. Berry, what songs are we going to play?"

He looked at me as if I were from Mars and answered, "Chuck Berry songs." He then picked up his guitar, started a riff and rocked right into "Roll Over Beethoven." I yelled to the band, "He's in C!" And we all jumped in as best we could. In the middle of the second song, he suddenly stopped playing and turned to me: "If you want to get paid, boys, you'll pick up the tempo." He lit into "Sweet Little Sixteen," and we rocked and we rolled.

After the show, we waited backstage to get paid, and we tried to talk with him. After all, he was our hero—*the one and only Chuck Berry*. Berry walked out of the promoter's office and handed us $500. "You did good," he said, then downed another beer. "Gotta go. Got another gig." He climbed into his big Cadillac, and as he drove off I said to myself, *Wow! Did we just back up Chuck Berry in concert? Unbelievable!* My dream fulfilled—at seventeen!

I got a regular gig playing at a bar in the black neighborhood downtown. We played four nights a week: four forty-five-minute sets, a fifteen-minute break between each. We'd play songs by Little Richard, Bo Diddley and Jimmy Reed.

When a popular out-of-town act would come in, we'd back them up—people like Wilbert Harris ("Going To

Kansas City"), The Platters ("Only You," "Smoke Gets In Your Eyes"), The Coasters ("Charlie Brown") and John Lee Hooker, the great blues legend.

We learned what a crowd liked and disliked—and fast. Instead of clapping or yelling, this audience threw beer bottles if you weren't pleasing them.

We must've been doing something right, because the Royal Playboys were soon signed to a major record deal with RCA, and we recorded our first song.

Unfortunately, we were signed to RCA just before the company changed presidents. As management went through an upheaval, more than a few artists were lost in the shuffle—including us.

It was a frustrating disappointment, and I decided to get an assembly line job with Ford, building carburetors for Mustangs. I was still serious about rock and roll; I considered Ford temporary—something to do until I could get into music full-time. I figured it wouldn't take that long. The job was security. What I didn't see at first was that it was also a trap.

It wasn't too long before our bass player committed suicide, and the Royal Playboys dissolved.

I formed another band and went to Illinois to back up teen idol Del Shannon ("My Little Runaway," "Hats Off to Larry").

Groups just come and go. It's usually because they can't seem to get along together—it's an ego thing.

Dutch Elm was the name of another part-time band I started. It was a horrible name, but the idea was that we

were a disease and we were spreading it through music. Hey, to us it made sense at the time.

It certainly didn't hurt us. Whenever a national act—like The James Gang with Joe Walsh, Steppenwolf, or The J. Geils Band—came to town, we were the local band booked to open for them.

There were other local rockers we played with who would soon go national too—Bob Seger, Mitch Ryder, MC5, and Grand Funk Railroad.

I even played again with Chuck Berry. It was at a three-day rock festival at the Detroit Fairgrounds, and 10,000 people were expected. Twenty thousand showed up. The rock magazine *Creem* ran a feature story about it by music critic Dave Marsh, who said, "Rockin' Reggie and the Dutch Elm were really rockin' the crowd."

The name stuck. Some people may not have known me by name, but they knew the name of Rockin' Reggie.

I was tapping into the rock scene, and that meant drinking more and taking drugs. I tried smoking hash to see where I could go. Others had made millions from the songs they said they got while tripping out—*why not me?*

A guy came up to me one day and told me he was a record producer. He liked my songs and wanted a tape of my songs to play for a group he was producing. It was Bob Dylan's backup group, The Band ("Up on Cripple Creek"). I thought this was the "big break," so I gave him my songs. But when I tried to call him, as he'd told me to do, his phone was disconnected and he had moved. I was never able to reach him, and he never called. But later I did hear one of my songs on an Ohio radio station, credited to someone else.

By this time, I had graduated from just playing the clubs to the larger concerts, and though I was just a front act, at least it was *closer* to the "big leagues." I was making a lot of contacts and friendships.

You never forget the people you meet during your "hungry years." So many of us were at the bottom, trying to find a way to make it, but I could usually pick out the ones who would someday be the stars. One guy that I especially remember had been with the Lourds, then the Amboy Dukes. He stood out from the rest. He used to say, "It may take me ten years, but I'm gonna make it. I'm gonna be one of the biggest stars in the world, and I don't care what it takes to get there. I'll never give up—never!" He was one of those "strong survivors" who stuck it out. His name: Ted Nugent.

Then one hot July day I was working in the factory, just like my dad, and for a split second I thought, *Well... maybe it might not be so bad to work here for thirty years and settle for a gold watch and a pension.* Then I couldn't believe I had even *considered* that.

When you're young and starting out, your hopes are high and you fear nothing. Then each obstacle you hit wears you down just a little. Nobody likes pain, and if you have the choice, you take the road that's easiest—until you discover you took the detour and you're not on the road you dreamed of at all.

But the ones who succeed—most of them—have so much desire that they'd rather fight through the pain. I

didn't know how much pain was ahead for me. If I had, maybe I would have chosen differently. But my desire to succeed was strong.

I remember, as a little boy, hearing about Buddy Holly, Ritchie Valens, and The Big Bopper dying in a plane crash. And it was there in the Ford factory, on the radio, that I heard that Otis Redding had just died in a plane crash too. They were all young and immensely talented and gave their dreams a chance. I wanted to give myself the same chance before I died.

The moment after I thought about working for that pension, a co-worker who had worked in a band with Jerry Butler ("He Don't Love You") began softly singing "Workin' On The Chain Gang." I knew what I had to do, or I'd be miserable the rest of my life. I walked over to him and said, "I'll see you later on the charts."

I walked out and quit that afternoon. Years later, I did see my friend David again: He was traveling with the Temptations.

Rockin Reggie

LIFE IN THE FAST LANE

Once upon a time in America when there was unrest—riots, drugs and killing—in Detroit, most people worked in the auto factory, making hardly any money.

Young people growing up under those shadows needed something to hold on to, something of their own. Many chose to take drugs, and music was a release for them. There were many nightspots where a kid could hang out, be seen or slip away to hide. One place was the old Grande Ballroom. It was a seventies' style psychedelic picture: weird clothes, lots of drugs, party, party, party.

There, on any given weekend, you could see Janice Joplin, Eric Clapton, The Doors or one of the local bands. I played there a lot with different bands.

That was where I got turned on to drugs and smoking dope. One night I found myself smoking a joint with Jerry Garcia of The Grateful Dead. (I'm not proud of it— it's just true.)

There were a few places we used to go: Ann Arbor, Birmingham, Michigan. Frigid Pink, Mitch Ryder, Iggy Pop, MC5, Ted Nugent, Bob Seger and some of the local bands ran together. We played at different clubs and ran from party to party.

One night I went with an old friend to Flint, Michigan, where the Grand Funk Railroad lived. We started out at their farmhouse and then went to a concert where Jimi Hendrix was playing. Hendrix was one of my guitar idols. I went backstage, and there were Jimi and his band sitting on the couch and waiting to go on stage. He had a drink in one hand and a joint in the other. I introduced myself to him. He smiled really big and said, "Hand me my guitar." He just started playing. *Wow!*

Then he said a few words to me, handed me his drink and the joint and walked out on stage. He played a few songs, and then he set his guitar on fire. It amused me. (Today I don't feel the same about destruction as I did then.)

My dream of being a rock star took me many places, including some places I never should have been. I worked for many years to be the "best," to work with the "best" and to have everything the "best" had. I can think back over those years and just pick out the high spots. It wasn't all glamour and good times, but some things stand out.

I remember when I met the Alice Cooper Band. I had met their lead guitarist, Glen Buxton, at a bar in Los Angeles, and we had really clicked. Before long they all moved to the Detroit area, and my house was only a few minutes away. We became pretty good friends—Alice, Michael, Glen, Dennis, Neal and their super manager, Shep Gordon, and me. I eventually worked on four different albums with them.

I met them one night when I was in Chicago recording an album with a blues band. I went over to say hello, and they asked me to help them on the song "Be My Lover." I

played and sang background vocals with them. It became a hit song. The album was called *Killer*. I also worked with them as a session guitarist on their album *School's Out*. Glen and I came up with the guitar riff on the song one night, just goofing off. It was an old Chuck Berry riff—just turned around. Glen was a great guitarist and my best friend. I worked on four songs on the album. My name was on it—"Rockin' Reggie Vincent, guitarist and background vocals." Alice was the one who changed my name from Vinson to Vincent.

It would be the first gold record for all of us and a dream come true for me. I wrote the music for the song "Billion Dollar Babies." Alice wrote the words, and Michael Bruce wrote some of the middle bridge. As on the other two albums, I played guitar with them and did background vocals. The English singer Donovan also sang on the song. It became number one in America and, I

Alice Cooper and Reggie receiving their first gold record for *School's Out*

believe, in eight different countries. We earned another gold record and our first platinum album.

I also helped Michael Bruce in Canada with some ideas on an album. But like most rock and roll bands, soon the end was near and everyone went his own way as the band broke up. I've heard a lot of stories about the Alice Cooper Band: some true, some not so true. We were buddies then; and after all those years, we're still friends.

I remember, like so many others, seeing the Beatles performing on *The Ed Sullivan Show* just as Elvis had. The fans went wild. *Wow!* I wanted to meet them.

Years later I was living in New York, doing a lot of session work. It was paying the bills, I was paying my dues, and I knew a lot of people.

I have a friend named Shelley Yakus, a recording engineer and record producer who worked with Lou Reed, David Bowie and many others. He asked me to sing on a track at his studio with Bobby Hatfield of the Righteous Brothers .

It just happened that Neal Smith was in another studio room recording his album *Platinum God,* so I got to help him a little bit on it and brush up on our old friendship. He is a super guy.

Shelley told me he wanted to introduce me to John Lennon. Shelley was doing some engineering for him: *Whoa!* Of all the Beatles, John was my favorite. Shelley took me into a studio room and I walked in. There he was—John Lennon. Shelley said, "This is my friend Rockin' Reggie."

"Rockin'," he said. "I like that." Then John said, "My bass player hasn't shown up, and I need someone to rock on my session. Do you play bass?" Well, I was no Paul McCartney on bass, but who could pass up an opportunity like that? "Sure, John, whatever you need."

John was drinking whiskey from a bottle and getting pretty high, sitting on a stool playing his guitar singing some "oldies but goodies." I followed along on bass and sang a little harmony with him. Harry Nilsson was jamming on the piano, and Peter Wolf of the J. Geils Band was playing some kind of percussion.

To my surprise, Paul Simon walked in the room, and John stopped playing. Paul walked over to him and introduced himself to John. John said, "That's cool. Join in with us." Paul sat beside me and tuned to my bass. John counted "1-2-3-4-Be-bop-a-lu-la-she's-my-baby"; then he went into "Slippin' and Slidin'" and "Stand By Me." I'd grown up with those "three chord songs."

There with the legendary producer Phil Spector, Roy Cicala, Shelly Yakus and a few other heavyweights, I saw this as the session of all sessions. The "who's who of rock and roll" were there.

After that, we cut three or four songs.

Then John said, "Hey, Rockin', let's go party. Hey, Harry let's go get drunk." So the three of us left the studio and jumped in a cab. Harry, John and I were headed out to the Big Apple. For three days and nights we never closed our eyes as we partied from one place to another.

We also got thrown out of a couple of places! John and Yoko got into a big fight over the phone, and Harry got in a brawl with someone. So I just played it low-key.

John took me over to meet Derek Taylor, his business manager. He was cool. We visited for a couple of hours.

John picked up his guitar and started playing some new songs, and then he went into some old rock and roll stuff. Then he said, "Rockin, go get another guitar from the other room." So I ran and got one. He began to sing his song "Come Together." *Whoa!* Then I asked him how he did that guitar riff, and he showed me. *Whoa! John Lennon of the Beatles is giving me guitar lessons!* I said to myself, *Nobody will believe this.* But it was all true. For some reason, God had a plan for me to meet John Lennon!

Everywhere I went with John, if people recognized him, they would start mobbing him. In just a few minutes there could be fifty people around him wanting his autograph. When I asked him if I could have one, he looked at me strangely and said, "Ok." Then he handed me his bottle of whiskey, and I took a drink. John was really cool to me.

I had told everybody—even my mom—how I had met John Lennon and played bass with him, so I waited for the album to come out. Possibly my name was on it?

No! When it came out there were two different versions. It only said *Rock & Roll,* John Lennon, produced by John. There was no Paul Simon, Peter Wolf, Harry Nilsson, Rockin' Reggie or the other three or four who played instruments on it—nothing.

I was mad and embarrassed. I had told everybody, and now it looked as if I'd been lying. But a few of us know the real truth. I asked Derek Taylor what had happened. He said, "It's only rock and roll, baby." To my surprise, someone sent me a gold record for my work.

It's sad that John's gone, Harry's gone and now Derek's gone. All of these men were great in their own right. Three days and three nights might seem like a short time when you meet someone, but to me it will be a memory of a lifetime.

If I had to pick one highlight in my years in the music business it would be the night I went to see Roy Orbison in a small club. He came over to my table, and we talked. He had a gentle, kind spirit.

We had never met, and he had never heard me play, but he asked if I would like to join him for a couple of songs. Roy Orbison had been my teen idol since I'd been twelve years old, and as a boy I had practiced his songs over and over, day and night. Here was my big chance. So I got my guitar out of my car, tuned it up and nervously got on stage. Roy introduced me to the small crowd.

Then Roy counted the song off, and his beautiful voice began singing "Only the Lonely." He was in perfect pitch, and so was the band. The crowd went wild and sang along with us. Then he said, "Do you remember this one?" He started his guitar riff off, *dun-dun-dun*–"Pretty Woman." It was unbelievable. He wrote his own songs, had the best melodies, his guitar riff, and the greatest falsetto voice there ever was.

Yes, Roy Orbison was my favorite memory. Chuck Berry was cool but slick. Etta James she could sing the blues. Del Shannon was "Unique." The Platters had great harmony: "Only You," "Yes, I'm the Great Pretender." I

believe I was the only white guy in the band. They were fun people. I was blessed in my life to have played guitar and sung backup vocals for them.

I met Marvin Gay and Stevie Wonder at a recording studio. I watched Marvin record the song "What's Going On," and I watched Stevie record one of his songs, "Fingertips." Both of them were generous.

Marvin asked me to play on his next session, and when the day came to record I was there setting up with producer Don Davis. But Marvin never showed, so I ended up working with a songwriter on a song titled "Spiders and Snakes." It was a silly song. But Jim Stafford helped him on it and sang the vocals, and the major label M.G.M. recorded it. It sold 1,000,000 records. You just never know about music. But it helps to be at the right place at the right time and know the right people.

One day I was in Los Angeles visiting Alice and Shep. Elton John came over, and we jumped into his limo. Elton was on one side, and Alice Cooper was on the other side. I felt I had arrived in the "big leagues."

But that day, just when life seemed so kind to me, tragedy struck. I got a call telling me my house in Detroit had caught on fire. I lost my recording studio, my original Bo Diddly guitar—the very rare Black Box one—my gold records, all my photos, my recording masters and some great photos of myself with a lot of celebrities that I'd played with through the years. Everything that I had saved was gone. That was a sad day. I had to rebuild and start all over again. I was really living "Life in the Fast Lane."

THE FRENCH RIVIERA

Perhaps I was burned out on drugs and alcohol. I don't know. But suddenly I found I couldn't write songs or even pick up a guitar anymore. I hadn't had a block this severe since my father had died; I was fighting depression almost constantly. If I could not create music, I felt I would die—physically, mentally and spiritually. Without a creative purpose, I believed nothing could keep me alive. I had to get away, and the French Riviera seemed the perfect antidote for my symptoms.

The night I arrived, half a world away from home, I felt as though I was drowning in absolute sadness. I had prestige and money; I ran with famous people; I'd had a hand in millions of albums sold around the world. But I didn't know who my friends were or whom I could turn to, and I couldn't trust anyone—maybe not even myself—even though I had made it to that famous place in life where the very best that money could buy was commonplace.

Have you ever been to the Riviera? The *ooooh-la-la* French Riviera? Music is in the air. The harbor lights reflect off of the most luxurious yachts in the world. James Bond (Sean Connery) stayed here. Here is where the most beautiful women in the world stayed, wearing the biggest

diamonds in the world, driving the most expensive cars in the world.

The boulevards are lined with small cafés that overlook the ocean, where the sunsets are so spectacular that photographers and filmmakers from around the globe can't wait to make another television or movie special right here. The Cannes Film Festival is held here every year. From all over the world, stars come to shine here: Paul Newman, Anthony Quinn, Sylvester Stallone and Jack Nicholson—every name you've ever seen on a hit movie marquee.

You can go through ten or fifteen grand in one week. So you see, to run with the *big* boys you have to have *big* money to spend. Otherwise, you won't get invited to the places the tourists never get to see.

In the midst of all this extravagance, I felt so alone—*so* alone. Have you ever felt that way? I had to get myself connected to something real.

In my hotel room, I dropped to my knees and prayed to the God I remembered from my childhood, the friend my mother always leaned on. I wanted to know if He would be there for me. "God...if You are really there... please help me. I don't know who I am—this Rockin' Reggie that I created. I'm so lonely trying to be *somebody.* I'm losing it all. God...if You are God...send me someone who will be a friend. Just a little help is all I need. If You do this, God, I will owe You one."

The words came from my hurt—a deep hurt—and I don't know now how sincere they were. Maybe I was just trying to cut a deal with God, trying to get through this void, this block that was holding me away from myself and everything around me.

Whether I was sincere or not, God always remembers the words we say to Him. And I guess He was serious, even if I wasn't sure—because around midnight, a voice woke me. *Reggie, get dressed and go for a walk.* I rose up with a start. No one was in the room. Maybe it was a dream. But now I couldn't get back to sleep, so I dressed and went for a walk along the Mediterranean shore.

Nighttime on the French Riviera is filled with party-goers and pleasure-seekers, laughter and music. I walked past it all, unseeing, lost in my own thoughts of where I was going and how I would get there. Some time and who-knows-how-many footsteps had passed while I considered how I might help myself—and how helpless I was.

I was so wrapped up in my own little nightmare that I bumped into someone: a music production executive from New York, Andy Hussakowski, who was on the Riviera for a music festival. He took one look at my face and said, "Let's get some coffee." Apparently, he had seen right through my "everything is wonderful" routine.

We walked a short distance to a small café on the water and ordered something. Andy looked into my eyes and asked, "Okay, Reggie, what's up?"

Before I had a chance to answer, someone stopped at our table. I looked up to see a distinguished gentleman, well dressed and wearing a diamond ring that would have blinded any jeweler. "Hey, Rockin'," said Andy, "meet the legendary Seymour Heller."

Heller had been a manager for more than thirty years, guiding the careers of Ginger Rogers, Doris Day, Lawrence Welk and many others. One client he had managed for all that time was the flamboyant Liberace, who had also found an unknown talent singing in a tiny little bar: Barbra Streisand.

Heller said, "I'd gone to bed, but something woke me up. So I came down to get something to eat." *Had he heard the same voice I had heard?* I wasn't about to ask.

We talked on until the sunrise about music, show business and people. He'd seen it all, been everywhere and done everything. Oddly, he seemed more interested in me and my plans than in his own past history. It was a pleasant meeting and a pleasant parting.

Over the remainder of my ten-day stay on the Riviera, we got together a few times: dinner; one or two evenings out and about; a visit to the Rolling Stones' 135-foot yacht, where I met their record producer and the producer of The Moody Blues. That was an outstanding band!

The last day he was in town, Heller called me over to his suite. "Reggie, I've cut down on my artist management. I've still got Liberace and a few others. That's about it. But I'd like to manage *you*."

Thank You, voice in the middle of the night! Heller manage me? Was he joking? How would a rocker fit in with Liberace's act? I had gotten my hair cut and was dressing less like a rock and roller, but I still didn't see myself in sequins. I mean, I'd been with Alice Cooper and KISS. That's quite a ways from the picture Liberace calls to mind.

VIVA LAS VEGAS

Still, when I returned to Detroit, I did call him. He flew me to Vegas and introduced me to Liberace himself, the man whose style of dress and showmanship was the pattern for Elvis and Elton John. Then Heller sent me to Beverly Hills to see how his company worked. We had dinner one night with his family—sweet Jewish folks who made me feel right at home.

He offered me a five-year contract as a songwriter and performer. He told me straight out it would be no easy road. "Liberace and I are partners. If you sign with us, you become part of our family. Behave accordingly. The same way I built Tom Jones and Glen Campbell, I'll work for you. You'll start small and sharpen your talents, and I'll open the doors for you. Waiting will be the hardest part."

I said, "No problem." And I signed on the dotted line.

So I moved to Las Vegas and found a nice home with a pool, and I began—one step at a time. "Starting small" meant working at the concession table, selling books and records outside of the show itself. Of course, we sold thousands of dollars in Liberace products every show; but I was still at the table and not on stage—or even in the audience.

I traveled with Liberace (his close friends called him Lee) in his private limousine, fetching and carrying. I even carried his hot-pink briefcase. Everywhere he went, I carried that hot-pink briefcase. It wasn't until many months later that I found out that hot-pink briefcase contained his personal jewelry: maybe half a million in diamonds or more.

Every show, he would say to his audience, "How do you like my furs? How do you like my diamonds, ladies?" Then he would laugh and say, "I hope you enjoy them, because you paid for them."

Of course, even working on the ground floor of the Liberace organization wasn't such a bad gig. Lee was a great guy to work with, and anyone who wanted to meet Lee usually had to go through Seymour and me to get backstage. So I met a lot of celebrities and Lee's personal friends.

One of Lee's best friends was Debbie Reynolds. The first time I met her, she walked into Lee's dressing room with two bottles of champagne and drank them both by herself. Seymour said, "She does that all the time." Lee loved Debbie Reynolds so much that he gave her one of his precious dogs.

Lee had four or five little dogs in his room all the time, beautifully groomed with little ribbons in their hair—a different color for each dog. Lee really loved his puppies.

Picture this: A stretch limousine pulls up to a high-class hotel, and Lee climbs out holding all the little dogs on leashes, wearing his $300,000 fur coat and a half million dollars in diamonds, with me in a suit carrying his hot-pink briefcase.

People just stopped in their tracks and stared. It was like a movie premiere celebrity entrance. But I loved it, and I couldn't get enough of it. A lot of people would have loved my gig.

I remember meeting Bob Hope and Bing Crosby, among others. But most memorable to me was Sammy Davis Jr. Sammy loved to spend money, but his first love was music—singing and dancing. One night when he came to see Lee, I asked him if he'd show me a dance step. To my surprise, he did. I remember he had a great sense of humor, and he laughed a lot. He was a super guy.

Another time, he was performing at the Sands Hotel, and I went up to his dressing room to say hello. He poured me a drink, and we talked a bit. "Sammy," I said, "I really want to meet Frank Sinatra!" And he said, "Doesn't everybody?!" I never met Frank.

I did get to see a side of Sammy that most people would never imagine. He was quite a gun fancier and quick-draw specialist. He strapped on a black, western-style holster and showed me some tricks, telling me he had starred in some western movies.

Seymour began to open other doors for me, though. He booked me into the Tropicana Hotel and the Sahara, both dates with a backup band of my own. Vegas was quite the affair, rich and sparkling and packed with big names.

Performing for a casino audience was an indescribable feeling, although it was nothing like performing for my boss, Liberace. The first time I had this honor was when Lee asked me to sing for him at his birthday party. I got my

guitar and sang two songs. Liberace gave me a standing ovation. Now, that was a thrill!

I may not have been on stage much, but I was getting more attention. EMI Records in England offered me a recording contract, but I asked Seymour Heller to get me a better deal. I remember bragging to Lou Rawls, telling him how I had asked for more advance money and a better percentage. Lou said, "Rockin', you better take what you can get. It might not be around tomorrow." He was right: It wasn't.

Seymour continued to open doors for me. In Las Vegas he hooked me up with movie star and songwriter Delores

Lee and Reggie, Lee's sixtieth birthday

Fuller, who had written songs for Nat King Cole, Peggy Lee and many of Elvis' movies, including *Easy Come, Easy Go; Clambake; Spin Out* and so on. Delores discovered and managed Tanya Tucker, securing her first recording contract in Nashville, and also managed Johnny Rivers ("Secret Agent Man").

Delores introduced me to her partner, Ben Wiseman, who wrote fifty-eight hit songs, including Elvis' "Follow That Dream" and "Trouble" from the movie *King Creole*, and many songs in the film *Blue Hawaii.* Ben also worked very closely with the legendary Sammy Kahn.

Ben took me to the home of record producer Jimmy Haskell, who produced Ricky Nelson's early hits. On the wall at Jimmy Haskell's I saw his gold record for the song "Hello, Mary Lou": That was where my love for rock and roll had started. Jimmy invited me to work for a while in his songwriting room, and I ended up staying the night there, where all those hits had been born.

That's the way the music business is: It goes around and around. You might think you're getting up there in the world, working with the big stars. Then one day, you meet your teen idol and suddenly feel like an unknown kid again.

I met Ricky Nelson one day. I told him his song "Hello, Mary Lou" was the first song I'd ever learned to play. He smiled and started to sing it for me. *Wow!* He was a natural voice and a natural talent. He shook my hand and invited me to his show, and a few years later he actually auditioned a few of my songs. We had a long telephone conversation. He liked my songs because they reminded

him of his early rockabilly days. We even talked about getting together to record my songs in Memphis and maybe even getting Carl Perkins to play a little guitar with us. I was so excited. But that New Year's Eve, Ricky Nelson and his band were all killed when his DC-3 crashed.

Ricky Nelson was a real rock and roll star! Like many of his predecessors', his life had abruptly ended before it had really begun.

This reminds me of another superstar tragedy. Seymour introduced me to Colonel Tom Parker, who was Elvis' manager and mentor. I wrote two songs for Elvis, and Seymour liked them enough to send to Colonel Parker, who played them for Elvis. Elvis really liked them. One song was called "Rock Away." Seymour and I believed he was going to work them up in his next recording session. But three weeks later, while I was on tour in New York City with Lee, the phone rang in Lee's room, and the voice at the other end said, "Elvis is dead."

Millions of people were mourning Elvis: They were very loyal fans. But I felt sad because his song "That's All Right Mama" had inspired me to get into rock and roll in the first place, and much of what I had tried to achieve was directed toward the same kind of fame that Elvis had. And I felt more too: I was living the same kind of lifestyle that had seduced him.

I could hear the same emptiness echoing in the hearts of the biggest stars; I wasn't the only one. Liberace was making a small fortune a week, but I could see that same emptiness in his life. He was warm and caring but very isolated, struggling constantly to keep to himself as much as he could, even though he was surrounded by many devoted people.

Life was one party after another, from Glen Campbell's penthouse suite at the Riviera Hotel in Las Vegas, to Siegfried and Roy's estate, where the parties were even wilder that Liberace's.

One evening, in the midst of this emptiness, I saw a beacon of hope. Seymour called and said, "I want you to have coffee with me. There's someone I want you to meet."

She was everything I expected from the legendary movie star and singer Pearl Bailey. As we sat and talked, she suddenly gazed into my eyes and said, "Reggie, your face is so kind. Someday you'll probably be a preacher."

I nearly dropped my coffee. "No way!"

She added her famous Southern belle accent to her words as she said, "I'm always right about things like this. Mark my words: God's gonna call you to be a preacher."

7
ARE YOU READY FOR THE PRINCE OF PEACE?

L as Vegas was home to me at that time. I had lived there for three years. I knew just about everyone in the music business. When I had lived in Toronto, Canada, my best friend was Nick Panaseiko, a top promoter in the music industry. He's the one who got KISS, Blondie and The Romantics, just to mention a few, on the charts in Canada and the Detroit area.

One night while we were out and about, Nick introduced me to Wayne Cochran. Wayne was an early shock rock soul brother who wore a long cape and a very big, white, bouffant hairstyle. He traveled with the C.C. Ryder Band, and they put on quite a show. Wayne had been around a long time, and I had seen him more than once when they played in Las Vegas.

About this same time I had met a showgirl, a star in one of the glamorous Hollywood revues that are so popular in Las Vegas nightclubs. She was a beautiful young woman, and we really thought we were in love. I went to Colorado with her to meet her parents, and we went to meet the parish priest. He told us that we needed to become Christians and get baptized. It seemed like the old gospel I had

grown up with was coming back around in my life. I started going to church with the girl once in a while, but I guess you could say my heart wasn't really in it.

Wayne Cochran was doing a show in Reno, Nevada, and I called him just to say hello. He began to tell me about Jesus and that the priest was right. He invited me to bring my girlfriend and to come and see his show in Reno. I have to admit that my mind was more on the girlfriend than on Jesus as we were driving together. My thoughts were on an intimate weekend with a lovely young woman, and a visit with a friend.

That night after we checked in to our hotel room, we caught Wayne in the middle of his show. One minute he would be on the stage; the next minute he would run out into the audience, jump up on someone's table and start singing, "Ginny, Ginny, won't you come along with me?" The crowd really went wild. It was quite the show.

Afterward, we stayed up talking until four or five in the morning. He was the first entertainer to talk to me about being born again. He even opened up his Bible and read John 14:6: **Jesus saith unto him, I am the way, the truth, and the life: no man cometh unto the Father, but by me.**

The lady and I sat there with our mouths open. *Whoa. Hold on a minute.* This was not what we'd come to Reno to hear.

The next day, Wayne even took us shopping in a Christian bookstore. This was definitely not the weekend I had planned when we'd left Las Vegas.

That evening while the lady was getting dressed to go see Wayne's show again, I turned on the television in our room and poured some champagne. Johnny Cash was on. He was one of the great entertainers of our day; he had really been around the block a time or two. He would be worth watching.

Just about the time the lady came in and sat down on the bed to watch Johnny Cash with me, Billy Graham walked out on the stage and stepped up to the microphone. He said, "Tonight, I'm going to talk to you about show business and rock and roll."

I laughed at him. "Listen to this guy! He thinks he can talk about show business, but he doesn't know anything about it," I said. "He's never played music in his life. He's probably never even listened to any rock and roll!" I was still laughing at him while I poured our champagne and we drank a toast. "I've got to hear this!"

Well, we listened. Billy Graham talked about the empty life of entertainers. He told how they had life around them but were dead inside. He spoke of loneliness, emptiness and sorrow. He read from an article about Elton John, who would perform every night for an audience of 20,000 or more and then go home to an empty room, depressed and unfulfilled.

Maybe this preacher did know what he was talking about. I had been around Elton John a few times, and he seemed to be a very lonely, empty and sad person. The lady and I looked at each other, then back to the television.

Suddenly, Billy Graham looked right at me, pointed his finger right at me and said, "You have got to stop what you

are doing. You are at the end of your rope. You must be born again. I don't care if you are in a hotel or motel. God will forgive you."

Well, just that quickly, I felt something catch at my insides, and I said to my girlfriend, "My Lord! We've been caught by Billy Graham."

"You must be born again. I want to lead you in a prayer of salvation right now. Pray with me," Billy Graham said.

I didn't think about how strange it was or how it would look to my friends in Las Vegas. I just got down on my knees and prayed that Jesus would forgive me, that He would come into my life and change it. My girlfriend was praying too. And peace—the clean sweet presence of the Spirit of God—entered that motel room and touched us both.

"Now," said Billy Graham, "go tell someone what has happened to you."

I went to tell Wayne Cochran. He didn't seem surprised; he just got out his Bible and began to teach us about Jesus and what salvation means.

He said, "You've got to be baptized." Wayne called a preacher and talked the motel room manager into opening the swimming pool. And then I was in the cold water once again, showing Jesus that I meant it.

It was just like that day in the creek in Tennessee—cold, cold water, a preacher's voice, Jesus and I—except for one thing, one small detail. Between that day in Tennessee and this day in Reno, Nevada, I had listened to a lot of other voices, chased a lot of different dreams, been hungry to make something of my life and make the big-time. This time when I came up out of the water, the only life I wanted to make something out of was His. I knew I didn't want to listen to any other voice ever again.

Still, I was surprised when He spoke to me so clearly and plainly I thought everyone heard His words: *Reggie, set my Word to music. And I will bless it.*

I asked the preacher if he heard voices. He looked at me a little funny, and I told him what I had heard. He said, "Son, there are three voices: God, the devil and yourself. Always be sure that the voice you're listening to is the voice of God, and you'll never go wrong."

Well, I guess that was about as much of a hint as anybody ever needed. I felt the Lord had laid out my entire life on a clear path, and I began to follow His voice. I prayed that He would let me meet Billy Graham, Johnny Cash and even Pat Boone—all the men and women who carried the gospel. I prayed that His Word would become real to other people through my music and that I would be a blessing to people all over the world, just as Billy Graham had been a blessing to me.

I had no idea how soon those prayers, too, would come to pass.

8

DREAMS CAN COME TRUE

I was staying in Las Vegas at the home of my friend Delores Fuller, with whom Elvis and Tom Jones had stayed. (Delores had written many hit songs for Elvis Presley.) One day a gentleman called there for me, asking if I would like to be a part of a Billy Graham crusade. God was answering my prayers again.

"May I speak with Reggie Vinson?"

"I'm Reggie."

"I'm Billy Graham's coordinator."

"Billy Graham? Why are you calling me?"

"Reverend Graham will be coming to Las Vegas for the first time in nineteen years to do a major crusade. Someone said you were saved and gave me your number. I was wondering if you would like to be Reverend Graham's chauffeur?"

I laughed. "I have gold records, I'm under contract with Liberace, I have my own driver when I'm in town—and you want me to be Reverend Graham's chauffeur?"

"Yes, I do."

I only paused for a second. "Okay." Then I covered up the phone and said, "Lord, is this what you do when someone gets saved: make him someone else's chauffeur?"

I called Seymour and asked if he would mind if I didn't go to Nashville with them.

The day came for me to pick up Reverend Graham from the airport. Besides driving, I was also supposed to roll out the red carpet. I mean, they really did have a red carpet. I was also given a chauffeur's uniform, including a cap. *I'll roll out the red carpet,* I said to myself, *but no way am I wearing that silly hat.*

When he arrived, security guards surrounded him, because someone had attempted to assassinate him before. I ushered him into the limo, and he asked me to wait a minute before going to his hotel.

I began to tell him what had happened to me in Reno: "Reverend Graham, I'm not really a chauffeur; I'm a rock and roller with gold records." I suspect this did not reassure him about my driving skills. But I forged ahead, telling him how I'd been in a motel room in Reno with this beautiful girl, and he had pointed his finger right at me from the television and said, "You've got to stop what you're doing! You must be born again!" Oh my Lord, I had been caught by Billy Graham!

He laughed and said, "God must have a sense of humor."

Just as I was about to pull away from the curb he said, "Wait just a minute. Someone else is coming." The car door opened, and in climbed the answer to my second prayer: "Hello. I'm Johnny Cash, and this is my wife, June."

I had to tell them my story too, and they both said, "Well, praise the Lord." Then Johnny saw the Gideon Bible on the seat next to me and asked if it was mine.

I told him, "Yes, I took it from the motel room where I got saved." He laughed. (I carried that Bible everywhere I went for years, until someone finally stole it from *me*).

When I told him and Reverend Graham how I had prayed that the Lord would let me meet them, and that they were answers to my prayers, they simply smiled. Reverend Graham said, "God does work in mysterious ways." Johnny and June said, "Amen!"

I joined Johnny Cash and June Carter Cash and her sisters for dinner three times so they could tell me more about Jesus. I was amazed at the way June prayed about everything. Johnny told me about his battle with pills and alcohol and how June had prayed so faithfully before he'd finally been delivered. She had never stopped believing for Johnny, and she said, "I'm going to pray for you too." A few weeks later I got a letter from them. They were real people.

Just like my mama prayed for me, I thought to myself.

During their stay in Las Vegas, Reverend Graham and his wife, Ruth, invited me to visit their home in Montreat, North Carolina. So one day I flew up to see them at their home. I had been invited to have lunch with Reverend Graham, but he had been called away unexpectedly. Mrs. Graham said, "I want you to come anyway."

So their assistant, Maurie Scoebee, picked me up and took me to their home. It's a beautiful log cabin home way out in the woods, surrounded by a large fence. When we pulled inside, Mrs. Graham said not to get out of the car: She would come out—and she did, with the biggest German shepherd I've ever seen. She spoke German to it.

Reggie and Johnny Cash

We went inside. Their home has the warmest feeling about it. She invited me to sit in Billy Graham's rocker, and she told me that Mohammed Ali had been a guest there the week before and had sat in that very rocker while Billy Graham had told him all about Jesus.

That afternoon we shared lunch and visited for about two hours. They had a guesthouse for me. The next morning she invited me to his private office in Montreat, where Mrs. Graham asked me to lead their staff in prayer. I was very honored and humbled that she would ask me to lead them.

After we had prayed, Mrs. Graham said, "Reggie, I'd like to show you something that not many people have seen. "These are the original tablets given to Billy by Cecil B. DeMille from the movie *The Ten Commandments*. Remember, Charlton Heston, playing the part of Moses, threw the first set to the ground and destroyed them. So a second set was made and used in the film, and they were given to Billy for his contribution as spiritual advisor for the movie."

There were many other things in the collection that inspired a deep emotion. It was a great honor to be allowed that insight into the character of such a great man. I believe Reverend Billy Graham has done more good for people than has any other person on earth.

For many years after that visit, whenever either Reverend or Mrs. Graham would write a new book, they would take the time to send me a personally autographed copy with a personal note inside. I have ten books that they have autographed and sent to me.

After my years of working with celebrities and top names in the entertainment world, I just took it for granted that I would always be around the rich and famous. I was already under contract to Liberace, whose name was a household word in every English-speaking country and most of the rest of the world.

I had prayed to meet Billy Graham, and I had prayed to meet Johnny Cash. I had prayed to meet Pat Boone—and when I met him, I found out he was my cousin on my mother's side. God is faithful!

When I found out how prayerful June Cash really was, and how gracious Ruth Graham really was, I knew I had to dig in to my new life in Christ with all my strength so that He could make me everything He wanted me to be. So I began to study from the Gideon Bible and to learn the words of Jesus and the people who knew Him. I attended many meetings and revivals.

I was still working for Lee, and I met a lot of people in gospel music who had always wanted to meet him. I got to know Mike Murdock, Roger McDuff and Dino Kartsonakis, and I introduced them to Liberace.

One day I read a Scripture that said a man couldn't serve two masters, so I went to Liberace and Seymour Heller and asked to be released from my contract. Shortly after that, I got a call from Dino Kartsonakis. He wondered if I would like to be on the PTL Show with Jim and Tammy Bakker, as his guest. That probably opened 300 church doors for me.

It looked like the gospel music business was going to be as good for me as rock and roll had been. I was doing what God had told me to do: putting His Word to music. I was following His voice, and He was blessing me, just as He had promised.

I'll tell you this story just to show you how God works when you believe. One day a guy with a trumpet came up to me after a convention in Chattanooga, Tennessee, and said, "My name is Phil Driscoll. I know you came out of rock and roll. Not too many people want to use a longhaired musician in ministry. Would you pray with me that God would open up a door for me so I could get some ministry jobs?" We held hands right there in that hotel lobby and believed God together.

Dr. Norvel Hayes had become a close friend of mine, and he invited me to stay at his home for seven days and minister at his school in Cleveland, Tennessee. Instead of going to bed at night, he'd fix us each a cheeseburger about one in the morning and keep us up all night talking about Jesus.

I taught at his school for five days, and then Kenneth Copeland came for the weekend and stayed with us in the little country house. God was all over that place. I was very blessed to be surrounded by men of such faith. I remember when Brother Copeland and I sang for Ronald Reagan's presidential election campaign.

Another time, I was at Brother Hayes' convention to share and sing with Ken Copeland, and Phil Driscoll walked in with his golden trumpet. He and I played a song together, and Brother Copeland said, "Phil, I want you to travel with me and do some conventions. That was the birth of Phil Driscoll's worldwide ministry. God had answered our prayer of agreement. Through the years Phil and I did a lot of meetings together. He is a blessing to be around and the best trumpet player I know.

Soon after that, moving to California seemed like the next step, and then it was time to look for a church. I was getting used to being a single man, without a steady parade of lovely ladies around me, but it wasn't easy. And the only thing that could keep that loneliness from being too much to take was the fellowship of committed Christians. As long as I was around people who were as sold out for Christ as I was, I was okay.

I wrote songs from the Bible, sang whenever someone asked me to sing, shared my testimony whenever I got a chance and kept following the voice of God within me.

I traveled a lot with Roger McDuff and Betty Jean Robinson, who are very sweet people and have become dear friends of mine through the years.

Roger McDuff invited me to Columbus, Ohio, for Pastor Bill Sharp's convention. This was the beginning of my ministry as God connected me with many great men of the gospel. Other guests at that seven-day convention were Reverend Dwight Thompson; The Happy Hunters; Jesse Duplantis, who had just come out of rock and roll himself; and Chico Holliday, an old Detroit rocker.

Fred Price taught us about faith and things he had learned from a book called *The Authority of the Believer* by Dr. Kenneth E. Hagin Sr. So I went out and bought the book, and it changed my life. God opened three or four other churches where Fred Price spoke and I shared my testimony and sang.

I started attending the Eagle's Nest, a small church in California, and met a woman—the only woman I knew, other than my mother, who was sold out for Jesus. She was the pastor's secretary and loved God as much as I did. We'd have coffee once in a while and talk. It was nice to have someone to talk to after having been alone for a while.

One evening we went to a Bible study at the home of some friends of hers from the church, and during prayer, one of the deacons began to prophesy over us that we were supposed to be married. Marriage is good—companionship and all. That would be good. We had heard from God, or so we thought, and couldn't wait to tie the knot.

After the ceremony, we moved to Charlotte, North Carolina, leased an old Civil War home and became regulars on the PTL show. I appeared with Little Richard and all of the top Christian entertainers. Efrem Zimbalist Jr. became one of my friends, and we did many television shows together.

I sang the gospel all over the country. I had appeared on over seventy-eight different television shows. My records were on the radio. Life was sweet.

We decided to move back to California. I was used to the life of a celebrity. Limousines, spotlights, money and fame were common to me. This impressed my new wife and led her to Hollywood. She was a beautiful woman. The enemy used her desire for stardom; and as the ways of the world began to creep in, we each took a different road. We separated.

"D-I-V-O-R-C-E" might have been good for Tammy Wynette's career, but it was a disaster for mine. Fearing I would "loose a spirit of strife and divorce" in their congregations, few churches were willing to open their doors to me. So, before too long, I couldn't get a singing engagement anywhere. So many pastors closed the doors to me. *Where was the love they preached?* I asked myself.

I did do a show with Jimmy Swaggart, but soon after that he started having some troubles of his own. The PTL Show got caught in a media crossfire, and it was no time at all before Jim and Tammy were out of circulation. And soon Swaggart would fall himself!

The divorce left me thousands of dollars in debt and emotionally and spiritually bankrupt. I realized that I had followed the wrong voice, but I couldn't seem to separate one voice from another. All I could hear were the loud voices of

failure, depression, loss, confusion and fear. I was a broken man with no direction. *Where is God?* I wondered. *Where?*

Kenneth E. and Oretha Hagin

LEARNING TO FLY

One day I was sitting at my Redondo Beach house in California when the phone rang. It was Reverend Kenneth E. Hagin Sr. We had met many years before through Lee Eller. Lee called him "Doc." Brother Hagin is his best friend. Lee is like an adopted father to me, and he had introduced me to Brother Hagin in Tulsa, Oklahoma. We had become instant friends.

Friend or no, it was like Moses calling me up on behalf of the Lord when Brother Hagin called and said, "Reggie, God's been talking to me about you."

Isn't it amazing how God will move someone across town or across a nation to call you when you need to hear from the one person whose voice you know you can trust?

"Are you okay? Are you in trouble?"

"Yes. My life's all messed up. My wife divorced me. It seems churches have closed their doors to me. I feel so alone. I've been praying that God would help me, but I don't feel like He's answering."

Brother Hagin said, "Reggie, you've been on my heart, and Oretha had a dream that you were in trouble. Why don't you bring your guitar and come out here to Tulsa and

sing for me at my world convention? I have something to share with you, and it needs to be done in person."

I hadn't sung in six months, but I said, "All right, Dad, if you say so. I love you and Mom; and if you think it's best, I'll be there."

When he called me up on stage to sing, I surely did not feel like it. But Dad Hagin had taught me about faith, so I stepped out and sang "He is the Way, the Truth, and the Life" just as I had when I'd first begun on my new road. The power of the Lord began to move in the building and, after the last note died away, I quietly moved to the edge of the stage and took my place there between Kenneth Copeland and Fred Price, both of whom I had ministered with many times before. There I stood, with my hands toward heaven, tears of repentance rolling down my face.

Suddenly, strangely, I felt as if I were floating in the air, not as a body but more like a presence. Way down below, I saw myself standing with my hands raised up. I saw a close-up of my face, and my eyes began to open.

Then in a split second I was back in my body, standing in a field of millions of beautiful flowers, a peaceful place, and looking toward heaven. Huge white clouds moved quickly by, revealing a big window covered with a curtain that was now pulled back. The window opened, and through it the most beautiful colors of the rainbow shot toward me. From the blue sky above, a bright multicolored beam of light came down heading toward me. It seemed to take forever before it hit me, like lightning, in both hands and went through them and down my arms, across my chest and right down through to my feet. Then, from the window, a white dove flew out. I could hear it making a cooing sound as it flew toward me. I could see it getting closer and closer—until it landed on my right shoulder. Then a voice out of heaven said, "I'm going to put it all back together."

The dove flew off into the sky. I heard the sound of wind and felt a breeze. The top of the rainbow began to fade and disappear. And I awoke.

There I was standing with my hands lifted up. Most everyone was gone except for an usher. I asked him, "Where is everyone?"

"They all left. You've been standing with your hands up like that for over an hour." I sat down hard in my chair. *An hour?* It felt as if it had been only a minute.

Dad Hagin walked up and said, "The Lord wants me to talk with you now." He began to say things to me no one in this life knew. I began to weep. I asked him if he'd ever had a vision: "Yes, many of them." I told him about the one I had just experienced.

"Reggie, you have a decision to make for yourself. Are you going to follow God or not?" I told him I was. Then he revealed something strange. "I know you're lonely and you may feel hurt inside, but the Lord has shown me that He has someone special for you. I know just what she looks like, the color of her hair and eyes. But I'm not going to tell you who she is or any of that. Don't run out and start looking for her. Wait on the Lord, and everything in your life will come together."

I went back to California, walking by faith, and started letting go of things in my life. I let my new Cadillac and my condo by the ocean go. I sold almost everything else. I cleaned my slate. Not knowing where I was headed in life, I went to Las Vegas to stay with my friend Delores Fuller. I waited on the Lord.

Isn't it just like the devil to throw discouragement at you after you have just received a blessing from the Lord? I was alone in Las Vegas, and deep depression began to torment me as the enemy tried to defeat me with things of my past. I picked up the phone and called my mama. I told her about Dad Hagin calling me, about the camp meeting and the vision and the word I'd had from the Lord. Then I broke down: "Mama, I feel like the devil himself is trying to take my life from me. I've been divorced twice! [After thirteen years of marriage, I had separated from my first wife, who now wanted nothing to do with me.] I've lost my house, my car and all my money. I'm so ashamed. I need a miracle, Mama."

"Son, let me pray with you. Lord, send my son a miracle. God, in the name of Jesus, send it right away."

We prayed, I thanked her, and then we hung up. A few minutes later the doorbell rang.

There stood a black man I had never seen before.

"Is Delores home?"

I explained that she was gone for the day and he should come back later.

"Hey, I think I know you."

"You do?"

"Don't you play guitar and sing?"

"Yeah, I sure do."

"You're Reggie...uh...uh...Vinson."

I nodded. I must have looked awfully down, because he asked if I was okay.

"I'm just having a bad day."

He stood there, and for some reason I asked him in. Within minutes, I began to share all the bad things that were going on in my life.

In return, he told me the story from Revelations 12 in which the devil torments a woman day and night until God gives her wings which enable her to fly to a place of refuge.

"Reggie, that's what you need to do. You need to put the past behind you, take those wings, and get on with your life."

"But every time I rise up, I fall down again."

"Brother, your wings aren't broken. You're just learning to fly."

He told me that when he'd been a little boy, about twelve years old, his daddy had taken him to the doctor. "They told us I wouldn't be able to run and play like the other boys as I grew older because of problems with my legs. But my daddy was a preacher at a little church, and one Sunday he brought me up in front of the congregation and told them I'd been given a bad report from the doctor. My daddy said to them, 'I would like you all to stand in agreement with me that, not only will my son run and play with the other boys, but that one day he will dance. Yes, that he will dance.'"

Just then this stranger I was talking to jumped up and began to dance like Mr. Bojangles. He had indeed become a dancer, he said, and worked in Vegas shows with Ben Vereen and others. "Trust in the Lord," he said.

"What's your name?" I asked.

"They call me the Midnight Preacher."

I told him about my phone call to my mama, asking God to send a miracle. "He did," I said. "He sent you."

I never saw the Midnight Preacher again. In fact, when Delores came home, she didn't know who he could have been. I've always thought he was an angel, and I thought a lot about him in the next few days.

I began to write these words: "Your wings aren't broken, son. You're just learning to fly." I called my friend Phil Driscoll to tell him about my new song, and we recorded it together in Cleveland, Tennessee. I took it to conventions with me all over the world and even to Louisiana, where I ministered again with Jimmy Swaggart at Reverend Gorman's convention. I took it to Africa, where I did eighteen concerts, some of which were with Pastor Ray McCauley at the 20,000-member Rhema Church in Johannesburg. I took that song to Capetown, South Africa, and it sold more copies in Africa than any other gospel song up to that time.

God had begun to really use me. Pastor Jerry Savelle called me one day from his church in Fort Worth, Texas, and asked if I would come to preach for him. I had been there many times before to minister, but this would be different, he said. He told me that he believed God was moving him away from his church to go out to minister and he wanted to go out to a mountaintop to seek the Lord. So I preached for him, and we had a great service. God touched many people.

Then, on Monday, Jerry came back and we had lunch together. He told me that he was going to turn his church over to Brother Harold Nichols, who had been Kenneth Copeland's pastor, and go out as a full-time evangelist. He got hooked up with Kenneth Copeland as an associate of that ministry and has been very successful.

God has a plan for everybody if he or she will just believe.

There were still a lot of preachers who wouldn't have much to do with me, but there were some who really stood by me. Dad Hagin was always there for me. And, through television, God connected me with some of the best role models in the ministry so that I could be encouraged. I did many meetings with Kenneth Copeland, Marilyn Hickey, R.W. Shambach, Dr. Lester Sumrall and Pastor John Osteen. They were great role models to follow—and maybe my wings *were* getting stronger. I was learning to fly.

GOING TO THE CHAPEL...AGAIN

No one wants to look too closely at things that hurt them. The past has too many sharp points. I had left a wife and three little girls in Detroit when I was living the rock and roll life. The few times I had seen her since, she'd made it pretty clear that she didn't even like me anymore. To tell the truth, it was uncomfortable for both of us.

But my mom had stayed in touch with my family. If you knew my mom, you'd know she is not the type of woman to just let three grandbabies walk out of her life. And by now, if you're getting the idea that Mama is a woman of prayer, you're right.

She had prayed for seventeen years for the Lord to save her son and use him for the gospel. Mom knew a lot about faith. I never thought she might be praying for my former wife Sadie and my kids. I never thought about them at all, if I could help it. Some things hurt too much.

I had been invited to appear on the 700 Club. I called mom and told her to watch me on television. She called Sadie. I hadn't seen Sadie in eight years.

Mom had told Sadie she needed Jesus. Sadie wasn't listening. However, she did tune in to the show. She was

shocked when she saw me. She could tell I was different: happy and peaceful. She wanted it to be true that I had made a new life for myself.

Sadie says, "I've always been a survivor. It's not something you're born with—it's something you earn. You're a survivor because you survive. It's like people say: All men are created equal (and they surely are in the eyes of the Lord), but what happens after that is what matters."

Sadie Bernice Spence was born near a coal mining town in Montreal, West Virginia, but her family moved right away to a farm in Tomahawk, Kentucky. Her dad was in the logging business. He was a religious man who took care of his family most of the time, because her mom drank a lot.

She had six brothers and sisters—she was in the middle—but they were hardly ever all there at the same time. One day the roof blew off of their house and her littlest brother caught pneumonia and died. He was about two months old.

Sadie never really knew her mother. She was not herself when she drank, and she drank all the time. Because of her mom's troubles, the children were passed from relative to relative.

When the timber ran out because so many people were trying to make a living in logging, Sadie's dad went to Detroit to find work in the steel mills, and her Aunt Sadie took the family in. She lived way back in the holler with no roads leading to her house. They had to walk, rain or shine, two miles each way to catch the school bus.

One day Sadie was dropped off at the mouth of the holler. She started walking, but suddenly it all looked unfamiliar. She turned back to the main road. But no one was around there either. So she headed to town, six miles away. There she was, this child in a little white dress trying to get home and going the wrong way because she didn't know the way. Finally, she sat down and cried, "I'm lost." Eventually, someone who knew who she was found her and took her to her Aunt Sadie.

Most of Sadie's childhood memories are sad ones. One Christmas, the only toy she got was a doll. It was really cold outside, with a lot of snow, and she took her doll out to play on the woodpile. When she ran in the house for a minute, she left it there. When she came back, the doll had been torn to pieces. The old hound dog had gotten to it. Her heart was broken.

Disappointment was a frequent companion in her childhood, interrupted only when she went to live with her favorite aunt, Nona, in West Virginia. She always took Sadie shopping; and for the first time in her life, she had nice clothes. She loved Sadie so much that sometimes she felt as though she was really her daughter—or should have been. But her dad found a two-bedroom apartment in Ecorse, on the outskirts of Detroit, and he called them—her mom included—to join him there. For Sadie, the hardest part was leaving Aunt Nona.

Sadie hated living in Ecorse, because now her dad was drinking all the time too, just like her mom. She was only thirteen, but she felt a lot older because of the abuse and neglect and hard times. She hated school too, because she was taken from a small school in the country to a very large public school in the suburbs. Even though she was a straight-A student and had been promoted twice, she was so shy and nervous about being at such a big school that she just didn't try to make it work.

Sadie wasn't allowed to bring home any friends—not that she wanted to. The one time she brought home her best friend, her mom and dad had been drinking and started throwing beer bottles at each other.

They had some awful fights. Things got so bad that she finally had to quit school so she could stay home and take care of her three younger brothers. Her older sister Cricket got married just so she could get away.

Sadie started looking for love elsewhere too. When she was fifteen, she met an older man. Not realizing the consequences of her actions, she became pregnant. Her mom and dad were so mad that she ran away with a girlfriend to Kentucky to have her baby. Sadie's parents found her, and her mom was with her when Debbie was born.

Soon after, her mom and dad separated, and Sadie moved back to Detroit. Just to get by, she took a job as a waitress. She was sixteen years old and all alone with her baby.

When I first strolled into the fifties diner where Sadie was working, I looked like a rock and roll James Dean. He sat down and ordered a cup of coffee, lit up a cigarette and asked, "What's your name, lady?"

"Why?"

"Oh come on, what's your name?"

"Sadie."

"Well, Sadie, where you from?"

"I'm from Kentucky. But my daughter and I live down the street now."

"You have a daughter? You don't look old enough."

"Neither do you."

I laughed. She had a lot of spunk for such a little woman.

She said, "I had her when I was sixteen, and I've been on my own ever since. What's it to you anyway? Listen, whatever your name is, I'm working."

I asked her for change to play the jukebox, and when she gave it to me, I punched up a Sam Cooke song, "Darlin', You Send Me." When it began to play, I glanced over at Sadie, and she gave me a really firm look that said, *I know your type and what you're trying to pull.*

I stayed late shooting pool, drinking coffee and smoking until she got off work at 2:00 A.M. "Can I give you a ride home?"

"I already have a ride."

I was determined to get to know her. I found out who was giving her a ride home and told him she already had a ride. So he left. When Sadie's shift was over, I said, "It looks like you don't have a ride home."

"Why?"

"Because I told him you already had a ride home and he was no longer needed." She was mad at me—but I did get to take her home.

Home for her was one room and a kitchen in a boarding house. She invited me in for a cup of coffee. We laughed and talked all night long while we listened to an oldies rock and roll radio station. Suddenly I said, "You wanna get married?"

She laughed and said, "Sure, why not?"

We got someone to watch Debbie, jumped in my best friend's car and took off. She wasn't yet seventeen, and I had just turned eighteen. You had to be twenty-one to get married. So we went someplace where they wouldn't know us or check too hard, way out of state, to Elizabethtown, Illinois, just over the border from Kentucky. We found a justice of the peace and told him we were both twenty-one.

There we stood, in an old wedding chapel about to be married. Everything was wrong about it—too fast and all—but we were two crazy kids who needed each other; and that, at least, seemed right.

We were married for thirteen years, through good and bad times. I was a dad to Sadie's daughter, Debbie, and we had two of our own, Renee and Sunie Joy. But soon the bad times outweighed the good, and I didn't see any other way out except for divorce.

After we divorced, Sadie went into a deep depression. For relief she went to the bars and found whatever else she could to make her happy. Her daughters Debbie and Renee got into drugs too, and little Sunie Joy really didn't have much of a mommy.

So one day Sadie decided to remarry. She thought maybe that way she could get her life together and give the kids a father.

But her health began to fail. Her addiction to drugs got worse—much worse. She was having so many medical problems, and those surely didn't encourage her to get off of painkillers or Valium. She was diagnosed with epilepsy, and then she contracted a blood disorder too. Over the next several years, she would have many major surgeries.

None of that stopped her from going to the bars and staying away for days, partying all over town. She was an alcoholic and a druggie, acting like a zombie and out of control.

Even though she was married, she certainly didn't act like it. She was not only ready to self-destruct; she was destroying Dennis' life, and after four years she divorced him.

She was dying. She knew that what she was doing was wrong. She wanted to change her life but didn't know how. She had inner senses that if she didn't turn her life over to a higher power she would destroy herself.

That was the point Sadie was at when God allowed our paths to cross again. I hadn't seen her in almost eight years. I'm not sure what I expected when I went to Detroit for Renee's wedding. I had heard that Sadie's health was bad, that she was drinking a lot and that she was even smoking, which I had never known her to do. She had always been a good wife and mother when we'd been married. I was the one who had done all the drinking and running around.

When I arrived for the wedding, there was Renee with her child-to-be and her husband-to-be. My stepdaughter, Debbie, was in the hospital giving birth to her first daughter, Jennifer. And my little Sunie Joy, who had only been three when I'd left, was now eleven and so beautiful.

And there was Sadie. She'd lost a lot of weight. Eighty-five pounds isn't much, even for a woman who's only five feet tall. But she was still the Sadie I had loved when she was sixteen. We sat and talked for a while.

When it was time for the wedding to start in the park across the street, I was the last one out the door. As I stepped onto the porch, I heard a voice say, *Reggie, I'm going to put it all back together.* It was the same voice I had heard in Tulsa! Slowly, it repeated, *Reggie, I'm going to put it all back together.*

Was Sadie the woman Dad Hagin had told me about? Of all people, was Sadie—whom I had known so long and treated so poorly—the one God meant for me all along?

I said, "Lord, is that you? I don't understand. Sadie doesn't even like me."

At the wedding, I gave Renee away. I stayed a bit at the house and then went to Mom's. We sat down and talked. She told me more about Sadie—how her health had deteriorated after our divorce. "I don't think Sadie is going to live much longer," Mom said.

When I returned to Las Vegas, I called Sadie. The divorce had nearly destroyed her, she told me. She was honest with me about going to the bars and about depending on booze and pills. She was smoking three packs of cigarettes a day, she said.

I asked if I could visit. She agreed.

We went to the Henry Ford Museum, as we'd used to with the kids on weekends. We talked a lot. Sadie could see that I had really changed, and I could see a change in her too.

One day, I called her from Vegas. "Sadie, have you ever thought about getting married again?"

"To who?"

"Me."

"No thanks. I was married to you for thirteen years, and that was quite enough."

"Sadie, will you just pray about it?"

"Yeah. Okay."

A few days passed, and I phoned her again.

"Sadie, have you ever thought about getting married?"

"To who?"

"To me."

"Okay." I guess she figured it was a little quick, but she already knew what I was like.

She flew to Las Vegas. Her plane was late, and we had to rush to the license bureau to get a license so we could get to the wedding chapel on time. We missed getting married on her birthday by ten minutes, but our eyes were sparkling with love and excitement. It really wasn't too much differ-

ent from our first wedding, which had been twenty years before. We were still two kids who needed each other.

I rented a truck and got what I had out of storage. It wasn't much. We headed across the desert to start our new life together—again. Only this time, I was sure God was leading the way.

Reggie and Sadie

ALL THINGS ARE POSSIBLE

For years Sadie had been suffering from epileptic grand mal seizures that were violent and frightening. Sadie's father had been a preacher, but she'd never been taught to pray out loud or told about the healing power of God.

As soon as we got married, I took our family to Dallas and put us all under the ministry of Pastor Robert Tilton at the Word of Faith Church. Robert Tilton was our pastor and our friend. I continued to sing and share my testimony wherever the Lord would open doors.

Dallas was the beginning of Sadie's Christian walk. I bought her a Bible of her own when we first got to Texas, and she took to Bible study like a fish takes to water.

She learned enough about faith to let the Lord deliver her from her three-pack-a-day cigarette addiction. She got baptized in the Holy Spirit and really learned to pray. And gradually she began to help in ministries to the homeless and prison inmates. She was learning all that she could—and fast.

But her body was still afflicted by the epilepsy, carrying unhealthy blood and many tumors.

One evening I began to share some Scriptures about healing with Sadie. I told her the story of Dad Hagin's healing. Then I showed her Mark 11:22-23, which speaks of the way God heals in answer to prayer:

And Jesus answering saith unto them, Have faith in God. For verily I say unto you, That whosoever shall say unto this mountain, Be thou removed, and be thou cast into the sea; and shall not doubt in his heart, but shall believe that those things which he saith shall come to pass; he shall have whatsoever he saith.

I also shared with Sadie some other Scriptures that she had now heard many times and explained to her how they applied to her and the health of her body. We talked about whether or not she was ready to be healed, because, I told her, "God is always ready to heal. The choice to accept it was hers.

"I know God heals today," I said. "He has healed me of many things. The power of God will restore you and make you whole if only you believe." I told her I wasn't going to let the devil steal her health anymore. While she was resting quietly in my lap, I began to pray: "Lord, Sadie doesn't know a whole lot about Your Word and Your desire to heal her, so I stand in the gap for her, in the name of Jesus." In prayer, I covered her in the blood of Jesus. I began to break the power of sickness over her, acknowledging that Sadie would live and not die, according to the Word of God.

An hour passed in prayer. It was now past midnight. I kept binding that spirit of disease and death and commanded it in the name of Jesus to let her go. My voice became hoarse, but I would not stop. I started singing, "Oh, the blood of Jesus that washes white as snow," over and over again.

At three in the morning I was still in prayer. "Sadie, you are healed by the power of the blood, in Jesus' name. You shall walk and not grow weary; you shall run and not faint." (Isa. 40:31.) Sadie appeared to be sound asleep.

Then it was five in the morning, and I had been praying for almost eight hours without stopping. I prayed that Satan and every demon that had ever tormented Sadie's mind with doubt and confusion would leave, and that Sadie would be raised up and healed.

About then, I felt the power of God move in that room. Sadie woke up.

"Jesus loves you," I said. "He has healed your body."

There were tears welling up in her eyes, and she sounded just like a little child when she said, simply, "I know."

Medicine can help a little, but God heals completely. Medicine alleviates the symptoms, but God cures the cause of illness. The doctors had done what they could for Sadie. Then I had done what I could for her. And God did the rest.

Sadie was completely healed. Epilepsy, tumors, blood disorders—all were gone.

Thank You, Jesus. By Your stripes, Sadie was healed. (Isa. 53:5; 1 Peter 2:24.)

Faith in our little family grew by leaps and bounds after Sadie's healing. Hebrews 11:1 says that faith is a substance. When someone in your family has been healed of an incurable disease by the power of God, you know that faith is something you can hold on to.

One day, I told Sadie, "I believe we can raise our family again."

"When donkeys fly!" she said. "You'll never change Renee or Debbie. They are grown up, married and on their own."

"Sadie, you have to watch what you say. The Bible tells us that whatever we confess with our mouths will come to pass." Together, we prayed to the Lord that we were sorry, and we began to claim our children for His kingdom.

To some, it may have looked like a tall order. Renee, our middle child, had been pregnant before her marriage, and the marriage was not a stable one. Drugs and other things of the world were involved. She lived a godless life and was filled with anger and rebellion.

Shortly after Sadie and I began praying for our children to be saved, I was booked to sing and minister at a small church in Detroit. The service was going well. There were about 100 people in attendance, and when I gave the altar call, six or eight people came forward. To my surprise, one of them was Renee.

She was high on drugs, and she began yelling at me: "I hate you! Where were you all my life? I needed you, and you weren't there. I had to live on the street since I was twelve because of you." She started to cry.

I put my arms around her. She just kept crying. After a while, she said, "If you'll be my daddy again, then I want Jesus to save me."

We both fell to our knees, and I told her how sorry I was for all that I had done—or not done—in the past. I asked her to forgive me. "I have changed, Renee. I love you very much, and I'll always be your daddy," I said as the congregation watched.

I led my daughter Renee in the sinner's prayer, and she was born again. God is so good!

After the service, I went to my mom's house and told her what had happened. We called Sadie on the phone long distance and listened to her tears of joy.

All things are possible with God! (Matt. 19:26; Mark 10:27.)

OTHER PEOPLES' PRAYERS

As Sadie learned more about the love of God, we both began to see His promises come true in our marriage, in our children's lives and in our own lives. He is faithful to watch over His Word and to perform it. One by one, our prayers were being answered.

I had prayed that God would let my new music be heard all around the world. From my neighbor just east, all the way around to my neighbor just west—all the way around the earth—I prayed that my new music for Him would bless people and encourage them in their faith.

And I knew that my mama's prayers were what had turned the tide for me. I suppose there is a praying mother or grandmother in the life of every person who has gone through the world and come out on God's side.

Even though I was in ministry full-time, some things still seemed to take me by surprise when I saw them up close. I had no trouble thanking Jesus for the prayers He answered in my life and my family members' lives. And I knew He answered prayers for other people.

I was waiting for a plane one evening with Little Richard. We were both scheduled to appear on the same television show and had planned to travel together. When our flight was delayed in Atlanta, we had to change planes. Little Richard went on one, and I stood in line waiting for the next available flight. I was carrying my Gideon Bible, as always.

Behind me, a drunken man yelled for everybody to hurry up: "Hey, preacher, hurry up! I don't have all day."

Finally I made it on to the last flight of the night. But the "no smoking" section was full, and at the back of the plane was the only empty seat—between a man smoking, drinking and playing solitaire, and the loud drunk man. I crawled over one and took my seat between them.

The drunk man looked at me and said, "Hey, aren't you the preacher?"

"I'm not really a preacher. I just like to carry my Bible."

"Yeah, okay, preacher." He then yelled for a stewardess to bring him a drink. I was going to be stuck next to him for an hour and a half. *Great.* I was praying that the Lord would let this guy go to sleep or something—just to keep him quiet. No answer.

No sooner did the plane take off than this man yelled for another drink. I hated being in the smoking section, and now I was next to this loud drunk.

The whole situation was trying my patience—so I tried the Lord. I opened my Bible and began to read. The drunken man poked his head at my chest and looked at the red print in the Bible.

"I know what the red print means."

"You do? What?"

"It means Jesus is talking there."

"You're right. How did you know that?"

"My grandmother told me."

"She's a smart woman."

"She died, and she's in heaven now." It was quiet for a moment.

Lord, is this why I'm on this plane—to witness to this man?

He drank his beer, wiped his mouth and said, "Preacher, let me tell you something. Do you know what I'm about to do?"

"No, I don't."

"I'm going to Charlotte. I've got a gun, and I'm going to blow my wife's brains out. I'm going to kill her lover too. Then I'm going to put that gun in my mouth and blow my brains out!"

My God, he's really serious. "You can't do that."

He said, really loudly, "I can do whatever I want."

I heard the Lord's voice say to talk about his grandmother. "How would you like to see your grandmother again?"

"Hey, I told you she was dead."

"I know. But if you kill someone and kill yourself you will never go to heaven and you won't be able to ever see her again."

"Preacher, for a week I've been drunk. I found out my wife is living with another man. I can't stand it. I'm gonna kill 'em. What else can I do?"

"We could pray for the Lord Jesus to change her." Even though I had never even prayed for anyone to be saved before, I just began to pray—and God gave me the words. Then I said, "And let's pray that God will change your heart, so that you won't hurt anyone and that you will be able to see your grandmother again. Repeat after me: Dear Lord, forgive me of my sins."

He yelled, "Dear Lord, forgive me of my sins."

Everybody on the plane heard him and turned toward us. One woman in front waved her hands in the air, saying, "Hallelujah, brother, hallelujah!"

I tried to get him to pray softer. "Sir, you don't have to yell like that."

"I don't?"

"No, you don't."

When we finished, he said, "Thank you for praying with me. But that man who's with my wife—I'm still going to kill him."

I thought, *Dear God, help me.* "No, you can't do that. Let's pray again: Dear God, I don't want to kill anyone."

He repeated after me—even louder this time. The stewardess came up: "Are you trying to cause trouble?"

"No," I said, "He's just getting born again. He'll be quiet." I looked at him and said, "God's not deaf. You don't need to yell."

Now he had two hands in the air praising the Lord over what was happening. We finished the prayer, and he said, "Is that it?"

"That's it."

"But, preacher, what about my wife? I want her back." We prayed one more time for God to change his wife's heart and for her to love him again. This time he prayed really quietly.

When the stewardess came around for a last call for drinks, she asked if he wanted a beer. He said, "No, thank you. I don't drink anymore. I'm a Christian now."

When the plane landed and we were getting off, he put his head on my chest and began to weep. "Preacher, thank you for saving my life." He smiled and walked away, saved by the blood of Jesus.

I never saw that man again, but I do believe that when he got home his wife was there waiting for him and, when this life is over, he will see his grandmother in heaven.

Isn't it wonderful how God connects people together when they have a need? Just when you think there's no help for you, help arrives. God is never late. If you think God is ignoring you, look around. Maybe you'll see your answer on someone else's face.

That man's grandmother sure did!

TO EVERYTHING
THERE IS A PURPOSE

Well, the devil is a liar. Actually, the devil is a dummy. He keeps trying to tell us that God isn't listening, that our prayers will never be answered or that we aren't worthy. Of course we aren't worthy on our own, but by the grace of God and the blood of Jesus we are. God works all things for the good of those who love Him and are called according to His purpose. (Rom. 8:28.)

Many years had gone by since I had prayed that the Lord would let my music for Him be heard all over the world. One day, when it seemed as though my prayers were never going to be answered again, I ran into an old friend of mine, Mac Gober. Mac is a former Hell's Angel who is now born again and serving God in a mighty way.

He shared a story with me, and it made me feel as if I were watching a movie.

Mac had been asked to go to Africa on a mission trip. In Kenya, East Africa, he would be speaking in many small villages, most of which were very hard to get to.

He had to fly for over twenty hours to get there, and two men were waiting for him when he arrived. One was

a missionary who spoke a little English. The other was an African tribesman.

Mac climbed into their jeep, and they drove for five or six hours out into the bush. Finally, they reached the end of the road. After this it was just jungle. Mac felt as if he were in a Tarzan movie.

He began to think about where he was and that no one he knew had ever been this far away from civilization, that he could die out here and no one would ever know about it.

When it was almost dark, they came upon a village of straw and mud huts. The little children ran away and hid when the jeep pulled up.

The tribes' chieftain met them as they got out in the middle of the village. He could speak a few words of English, which he had learned from another missionary some time before. He invited Mac, his guides and the tribal witch doctor into his hut.

The huts have very small doors close to the ground to prevent wild animals from entering on all fours. Mac had to crawl inside on his hands and knees, and it was very dark inside. There was a small fire in a central fire pit; and when Mac began to straighten up, the first things he saw were some pictures on the wall. There, right in front of him, was a magazine picture of me, Reggie Vinson, playing my guitar!

He grabbed his chest and pointed at the picture. "I know that guy," he cried out. "That's *Reggie!*

The chief and the witch doctor both began to jump around and yell and gesture wildly. "You know him?" They began singing something in their native language, and for a moment Mac Gober thought he really was going to be killed out there in the bush country.

Then the chief settled down a bit and began to explain. He said that missionaries had brought them Christian magazines when they'd come to tell of this God, this Jesus. He'd cut the pictures out and hung them on his wall. He said he had prayed, "If there really is a God, as these missionary people say, let Him send me this man or someone who knows this man. Then I'll know there really is a Jesus who answers prayer."

He jumped in the air, spun around dancing and joyfully told Mac Gober, "Now I know there really is a Jesus, a God who answers prayers."

Now, God didn't have to go through all that to take the gospel to these people: sending Mac Gober to the middle of Africa to prove to a witch doctor that God does exist. God works in many ways to spread the message of His kingdom. He uses my music, just as I asked Him to, sending it all over the world. He turns everything to the

Reggie in Africa

good. If we just stay in faith and believe, then everybody gets blessed.

Soon afterward in Tulsa, Oklahoma, I met a couple from England. One of them said, "Hello, Brother Reggie. We really enjoy your music, and my brother in Germany listens to your tapes during the Bible study they have every week. Your music has blessed England and Germany."

God never fails to amaze me. He never forgets your prayers.

The confession of faith does work for more than just salvation and healing. The same verses Sadie and I had been standing on when I'd prayed for her healing, Mark 11:22-23, have been proven many times in our lives and the lives of others.

The need doesn't have to be life-threatening. The truth applies to every situation. If you ask in accordance with His will, He will move—as long as you don't stop believing.

When I started writing songs out of the Bible, I pretty much switched from rock and roll to all types of music. To me a song is a message to someone else. If you're going to hum a little tune all day, let it be an uplifting Scripture. After all, in order for the Word of God to work mightily in you, it first has to get in there.

The highest honor a country musician can receive is to play the Grand Ole Opry in Nashville, Tennessee. One morning I went to breakfast with Pastor Charlie Cowan, from Faith is the Victory Church, where I have ministered for him. I told him my vision of playing the Opry, and I read Habakkuk 2:3:

For the vision is yet for an appointed time, but at the end it shall speak, and not lie: though it tarry, wait for it; because it will surely come, it will not tarry.

He said, "Brother Reggie, I believe you'll do that." So I wrote my vision.

I asked the Lord to let me play the Opry. I didn't talk about it; I just believed that God would bring it to pass. Well, one day I did mention to another preacher that I was going to be on the Grand Ole Opry. He asked me when, and I told him I didn't know but that I would keep confessing it and believing God for it, and it would happen.

About a year went by and I still hadn't appeared on the Opry, but I kept saying to the Lord, "I'm going to be on the Grand Ole Opry, and when I do, Lord, I'm going to give an altar call so people can have an opportunity to be saved."

Now, if you've ever watched the Grand Ole Opry, you'll understand that an altar call would not be on their regular schedule. Maybe it's because most people in the South already know about Jesus. I don't know. Gospel music isn't avoided on the Opry: It just isn't on the regular menu, so to speak.

Well, that preacher asked me if I had been on the Opry yet, and I said, "No, not yet—but soon." He just shook his head. Many people don't believe until they see something for themselves (and sometimes, not even then).

Three more years passed before I saw that preacher again. Again he asked, "Have you appeared on the Grand Ole Opry yet?"

"No, not yet, but I will," I told him.

Some time after that, I was invited to sing and share my testimony at a really small church in Tennessee. After the service, a little old lady came up to my record table and asked how much my records cost. When I told her, she said she wanted one copy of each of my three albums, and she counted the money out of her little change purse onto the table.

Then she leaned toward me and whispered, "Sonny, have you ever thought about playing the Grand Ole Opry?"

"Yes, ma'am," I said. "I've been praying to the Lord about it for over three years."

"Good!" she said. "Because I book the guests for the Opry, and I want you to be on the show."

I almost fell to the floor.

We checked my calendar and agreed on a date. Of course, I was available.

When the day finally arrived, I flew to Nashville. A limousine met me and drove me to a beautiful hotel. I met with the music director and orchestra conductor, and we chose two of my songs: "He Is the Way" and "You Must Be Born Again."

Then they came to me and told me that the schedule had been changed and I was not going to be an opening act—I was going to be the headliner, the main act.

That night there was a full house. Miss Minnie Pearl came and introduced herself to me and then went on stage and introduced me.

I walked out on stage. The cameras were rolling. I was very nervous, but I made it all the way through the first song, "He is The Way."

I had begun to sing my second song, "You Must Be Born Again," when the Lord brought back to my remembrance the promise I had made to Him: that I would be a witness for Him and give an invitation for people to give their hearts to Jesus and be saved. For just a moment I thought, *Lord, I don't want to make these folks angry. I might want to play the Opry again someday.* But I had promised Him, and I don't make any promise lightly.

Right in the middle of the song, I said, "Stop the music." I began to share what God had done for me. The producer of the show started waving his hand at me, motioning me to start the song again, pointing to the cameras that were still rolling. He was mouthing the words, *"Don't do that!"* But I kept on witnessing about Jesus. Minnie Pearl was standing at the side of the stage

Reggie at the Grand Ole Opry

watching me when I asked, "Does anyone here want to be saved?" Forty-seven people stood up and said they wanted Jesus to come into their hearts.

I asked Jimmy Snow to come over and pray for them, and I walked toward the stage exit. I wasn't too sure what to expect, as angry as that producer seemed to be.

Still, I had kept my promise and been obedient to God. And He had drawn forty-seven people out of the audience into salvation. So if the people there at the Grand Ole Opry never let me sing on that stage again, I knew I was still way ahead.

But there were Minnie Pearl and the nice little old lady from the church in Tennessee, both waiting to hug me and ask, "When can you be on the show again?"

Wow! I thought. *What can I pray for next?*

14

PINNING THE WORD
ON THE DEVIL

I know that the work of the Lord is serious. Mistakes can be costly, because peoples' souls hang in the balance. The message of truth is eternal. But despite the seriousness of eternal, spiritual matters, I believe God has a sense of humor and He laughs. It's good to have a little fun once in a while. One of the songs I wrote takes a children's game and applies it to a not-so-funny situation.

> Well, when I was a child
> I played all those childhood games
> And my mama taught me
> How to pin the tail on the donkey.
> But then she taught me about Jesus
> And I've never been the same.
> I started going to church
> Learning the Word with believers,
> And started applying the Word.
> I found the devil a deceiver.
> Then I found out
> God's power lives in me.

It's called "Pin the Word on the Devil,"[1] and I'll admit that it calls up a pretty silly mental image. But Sadie and I have found it to be a very effective way to live. When the enemy of life tries to stop us from doing what we know God wants from us, we go to the Bible, find one of God's many promises and wear it like a suit of clothes until it comes to pass.

The only weapon the devil really has are the words he whispers to our minds. And the only words he knows all add up to lies: There is no truth in him. (John 8:44.)

So whenever it looks as if something is about to go very wrong, we just turn to whatever is pure and lovely and has a good report. (Phil. 4:8.) Every time you look there, you'll find Jesus.

Now, that's pinning the word on the devil!

Sadie will tell you how God's Word has changed things for us:

> Because we were young and inexperienced and didn't know we could lean on God, our divorce had been inevitable. But it had also been selfishness. I'd gotten tired of my marriage, and for my own self I ended it. If I could have seen the pain and suffering my children would go through because of it, I never would have put them through that.
>
> Debbie got married at eighteen, had two children and was doing drugs—even selling them. She probably had never seen me completely sober for any length of time at all.

Renee tells me that the only time I ever accused her of being high was when she was straight. She hated me and blamed me for the divorce. She was devastated. She was pregnant—and a drug addict—at seventeen. Her daughter is named Crystal—not for her beauty, though she is indeed beautiful, but for the drug, crystal meth.

Sunie Joy had her first child when she was sixteen. She had three by the time she was twenty-one. In the South when I grew up, if you weren't married by age fifteen, you were considered an old maid. It's different now.

Just about everything is different now, especially in our family. Renee gave her life to Jesus as her daddy led her in the prayer of salvation. She traveled with us to Dallas and on to Phoenix, where she was our praise and worship leader for many years, until she relocated.

My oldest daughter, Debbie, came to visit us in Tennessee and saw for herself the great change in our lives—especially mine. The power of God had delivered me from drugs and alcohol and healed me of epilepsy. This was such a strong witness to her that she dedicated her life to Jesus. She and her family then joined us in Tennessee and, like Renee, moved with us to Phoenix. Debbie was our secretary for many years, until she relocated to Texas.

Our faith in God gave us the opportunity to go to church with our family and raise our children again, just as we had asked.

Our youngest daughter, Sunie Joy, was the last one to dedicate her life to Jesus.

With God's help, my three children are teaching their children a better way. I trust they, also with God's help, will follow that way.

And Reggie and I are different too. About the only things that are the same are our names. This time our marriage is based on God and the love of God. We never argue. There's nothing to argue about. Now we know how to work things out—together, with God. We have a total partnership now. That's what marriage should be.

We even write songs together, joyfully. Music used to be the thing that tore us apart. Now it's one of the sweet things we share. And it is sweet.

Reggie and Family

FRESH WATER

On a hot day there is nothing like fresh water. Whose idea was that? God is a dream maker, and He has a dream for you and me to fulfill.

Many people have started out with a dream—a good idea, a word from the Lord—and it has burned in their hearts. But the longer it has taken, the less their hearts have burned for it. Finally they have let their dreams slip right threw their fingers. There is nothing more tragic than this.

Your dream—your vision, your word from the Lord—is the very purpose for which you were born into this world. You were born to be remarkable, just as God created us all to be. There is no one else in the world like you: Your fingerprints, your blood type, your individual personality and your specific eye color are unique.

It doesn't matter if your dream is a little odd or different. My family were farmers and factory workers. I dreamed of singing, songwriting, learning to play an instrument and having a gold record.

My stepfather went to college and dreamed of being an architect, and he did it. But when he married my mom he was afraid he couldn't provide for our family. So he got a

job making cars in a factory, and he lost his dream. He was afraid to set out, and forty years passed. All he got when he retired was a small pension and a gold watch.

That almost happened to me. I had a family, got a secure job and was afraid to leave it. One day after five years, I stepped out in faith and became a dream maker.

You have to watch out for dream robbers; they'll talk you out of your dreams. You need to be a dream maker. God made you to succeed.

When you take the big leap of faith from where you are to where you want to be, your dream can look like it's a long way off. But you can make it, and when you succeed, "O Happy Day"!

I'd rather be walking on the water with Jesus than rocking in the boat with Doubting Thomas.

Today I realize my dreams have not merely come true but have extended far beyond what I could have ever imagined. Challenging dreams that come to us from God breathe His very life into our beings. If you have His life and His dream, you have everything! "Your old ones will dream dreams, and your young ones will see visions." (Joel 2:28.)

When God first began to put the desire into my heart to pastor, I resisted. I thought this couldn't be God. I had a beautiful home in the hills of Tennessee. I was traveling all over the world. I had five gospel albums out and money in the bank.

But God had a dream of his own, and He used me.

God had kept me in touch with some of His dream makers: Dr. Kenneth Hagin Sr., Kenneth Copeland, Marilyn

Hickey, R.W. Shambach, Dr. Lester Sumrall and Pastor John Osteen. These were just a few of God's chosen people He hooked me up with.

It was through Dr. Sumrall that I met Rod Parsley, who is the founding pastor of World Harvest Church in Columbus, Ohio. He invited me to sing and share my testimony at his church when there were only about 150 members or so. We became very good friends. I used to stay with him at his mom and dad's home when Rod and I were both bachelors. I have ministered at his church many times since then.

Dr. Sumrall married Rod and Joni. I preached at Rod's church on a Wednesday evening, stayed that week and sang with Phil Driscoll at Rod's wedding on Friday night. Brother Rod was always a blessing to me.

I thought I was doing all right promoting the gospel right where I was, so I wanted to make sure pastoring was God's plan and not mine. So I went to see my friend and mentor, Dad Hagin. He was having a convention. When I arrived he gave me a seat in the second row. Not too long after, Brother Kenneth Copeland came and sat beside me.

"It's good to see you, Brother Reggie. I've come here to hear from God," he said.

Just like me, I thought.

Dad Hagin began to preach. About forty-five minutes into his message he stopped right in the middle and said, "Yes, Lord."

"Those of you who are in full-time ministry, the Lord has a word for you. So if you'll just kneel down right there beside your chairs..."

Brother Copeland and I just looked at each other and smiled. We both knelt down and began to pray. In a few minutes I heard the Lord begin to speak to my spirit: *Reggie, I want you to go back to the desert and bring fresh water to my people, for they are hurting and broken-hearted. There you will build their faith and uplift their spirits and begin a new work for Me.*

After the convention, I went back home to Tennessee to tell Sadie. The Lord had already prepared her heart. When I began to share with her, she said, "I already know. The Lord spoke to my heart while I was washing dishes. He said, *Soon I will move you from here to begin a new work for me.*"

We told the kids that God had spoken to their daddy's heart and we were going to move to Phoenix, Arizona, to be pastors. We joined hands as a family and prayed that we would all be in agreement.

And we were.

The next morning, Friday, I put a small ad in the newspaper and then went out to my garage and made a "for sale" sign and put it in our yard. My neighbor came over and asked if we were moving. I told him, "Yes, we're going to Arizona to start a new church."

"I hope you have better luck than mine," he said. "I've been trying to sell my house for nine months, and I haven't got a buyer yet."

"I'm not going to sell it. The Lord's going to sell it," I said.

He just looked at me.

Monday morning, three days later, a lady called saying that she had heard that our house was for sale. She and her husband had been transferred from Dallas to Tennessee and had been looking for a house for six months while they lived in an apartment with their two children. I told her we had lived in Dallas, and she asked if we had gone to church there. I told her we had gone to the Word of Faith Church. "We were there too," she said. "What's your name?"

"Reggie Vinson," I told her.

"Oh, my goodness!" she said. "I know you. I have all your music tapes."

She and her husband came to look at our house. It was perfect for them, right down to the colors of the carpets and drapes.

We also had a Dalmatian named Lady. I had taught her to bow her head whenever someone would pray. She was a "good Christian" dog. She was a part of our family. However, we didn't know where we would be living in Arizona and it would be a long trip and hot in the desert, so we all felt it would be better if we could find a new home for Lady.

I asked the lady if she knew of anyone who might want a good Dalmatian, and her children started jumping up and down. It seems they had been praying for a house *and* a Dalmatian. So Lady got a new home—in her old home.

That's just the way God works. Those people got a new home, and their prayers were answered. And we sold our home in one weekend. There was no strife, no confusion—just God.

That evening I went out to pull up the "for sale" sign, and the neighbor came over. "Oh," he said, "you decided not to sell."

"No." I told him. "God sold it for us already."

The man just looked at me. Then he said, "Maybe I need to ask Him to help me sell mine."

So we packed up. I drove the moving van, and Sadie and the kids followed me in our car. We found a place in Phoenix; a pastor in the area was moving and needed someone to lease his home. Then we rented a hotel banquet room to hold services in, and we ran an ad in Saturday's paper.

The first Sunday, we put out fifty chairs. Eleven people showed up at our first service. We had to walk through the hotel bar to get to the banquet room for our Sunday service. I led the singing and the preaching, Sadie passed the plates for the offering, and our daughter Renee did a lesson for the children.

I preached "All Things Are Possible—If You'll Only Believe" (Brother Hagin's message) as though there were 500 people in attendance. It had taken me two hours to copy his notes; it took me fifteen minutes to preach. It was quite an experience for all of us.

God will always show Himself mighty to accomplish His purpose. That first Sunday morning I put $50 in the offering basket, Sadie put $20 in, and Renee put $10 in. After church when we counted, there was $138 in total. The banquet room rent for that Sunday was $250, and the newspaper ad was $90. The numbers just didn't add up. We were already in the red.

So we prayed, and we asked God to help us do what He had sent us here to do. The next day our friend Pastor Robert Tilton called. He told me that he had felt the Lord dealing with him the night before and that he wanted to help us. He said he wanted to send us $1000 every month for the next three years to help us get our church started. It was just the miracle we needed.

Pastor Tilton sent that every month faithfully. He is another dream maker.

See? That's how God is. He takes the impossible and makes it possible.

Our youngest daughter, Sunie Joy, was fourteen the year we started the church. We sent her to a Christian school. Her class went on a weekend retreat, and she seemed different when she got back. Soon after, she told us that she had become pregnant that weekend. It was quite a shock to us.

I had to go in front and tell my congregation that my fifteen-year-old daughter had made a mistake. Sadie and I were so embarrassed. I felt that I was a bad example, and for nine months the devil tried to get me to quit and move away.

The Christian school removed Joy and her boyfriend, Russ. Russ was a track star and a good student, but the school showed no mercy.

God does, though, and He turned it all around for His glory and the young peoples' good. After the baby was born, the principal called and told Russ and Joy that the school had been wrong and that they were very sorry. The

kids went back to school in the eleventh grade and graduated a year later with honors.

Then, two years later, the school invited Russ to
preach at one of their services. God had shown Himself
strong on behalf of our kids, and all the kids at the Christian school got the benefit of that strength.

Sunie Joy and her husband, Russ, arc the youth
pastors at Family Harvest Church today. In addition to
their daughter, Natalie, they have two boys, Logan Elijah
and Connor Abraham.

When each of the boys was born, the complications
were so severe that the doctors feared we would lose both
mother and baby. Sadie and I knew by then that God's
report is one of life and health, not death. We prayed; we
spoke life into those babies and their mother; and we kept
believing in God and His Word.

Today the boys are healthy, energetic and intelligent,
and we believe they will both grow up serving the Lord in
ministry. Like their parents, they will be dream makers.

Studies have shown that child prodigies are not born;
they are developed. In each of us there is incredible,
untapped potential.

It's really simple—you choose your dream, and then the
dream will shape your future and your life. And if you've
chosen to follow God's dream, He will shape your future
and your life into victory. I know this is true. It happened
to me.

My mother had a talent. She passed it on to me. She gave
me my first guitar lesson. She believed in me. Dreams start
coming true when someone cares about you. I remember

her very words: "Son, all things are possible if you believe."
I never knew those words were in the Bible until I became
born again and Dad Hagin showed me where they were
found: Mark 9:23.

I guess you could say, "If you see it, you can have it."
Or you could say, "Faith is like a dream that you must want
so badly that someday, somehow, somewhere, sometime,
you know you shall have it."

Even though you make mistakes, it is better to try than
to never make a mistake.

Ex-heavyweight champion boxer Ernie Shavers (81
wins, 78 knockouts) started coming to our church in
Phoenix. I became his pastor and was best man at his
wedding. Ernie told me when he fought Muhammad Ali
for the heavyweight title, every time Ali hit him it was like
walking into a brick wall. But he just smiled at Ali and
came back stronger than before. He fought Ali two
separate times, and each time he lost by one point. When
people asked Ali, "Who was the hardest hitter in your
boxing career?" he always said, "Ernie Shavers. He hit so
hard I never thought I would get up. But I did."

Sometimes that is how life seems: We get hit so hard
that we never think we'll get up. But with God's help,
most of us *do!* In fact, God's desire is to make sure that we
do get up and go on with Him. Jeremiah 29:11 NIV says,
**"For I know the plans I have for you," declares the
Lord, "plans to prosper you and not to harm you,
plans to give you hope and a future."**

Many years ago I met a guitarist and songwriter who
came from Colorado. He was a great guy with a lot of

dreams. He had a drive to succeed. One day, he was at a recording studio trying to sell some songs. I recorded one of his songs, titled "Please Daddy," and it was a local hit. The next time I saw him he was on his own television show. His name was John Denver. John was a rare gem. Even today his songs are heard all over the world.

I really believe that good things come from God and that God gives you the talents to make them come to pass.

I have a good friend who has been blessed as a pianist and songwriter. One night we were writing a song together, and Donna Douglas came by. She played Ellie May Clampett on the *Beverly Hillbillies.*

We ended up having a Bible study, and Mike read a verse to us: **Write the vision and engrave it so plainly upon tablets that everyone who passes may [be able to] read [it easily and quickly] as he hastens by** (Hab. 2:3 AMP).

Today he writes his vision and dreams everywhere. He's one of America's best motivational speakers, Dr. Mike Murdock.

I told Donna Douglas about Dad Hagin's Bible school in Tulsa, Oklahoma. One day she moved to Oklahoma and later graduated from his Bible school. Today she is an ordained minister of the gospel and travels extensively, speaking.

As Dad Hagin taught me and many other teachers, preachers and psalmists, Mark 11:24 says, "If you'll not doubt in your heart but believe, you shall have whatever you say!"

Your victory is just ahead. Don't be afraid to step out. Where does the energy to take that step come from? First, it comes from faith in the One who made it possible. It comes from a positive attitude. It's a powerful tool. It starts with one small decision that blossoms into something beautiful.

Don't let negative thinking limit your potential. When you pray for each one of those ideas you have, pray that God's power can make the impossiblity a reality. I heard someone say that God has no wastebasket.

You keep your faith in God, and God will supply the power. And together you'll win.

Now unto him that is able to do exceeding abundantly above all that we ask or think, according to the power that worketh in us.

Ephesians 3:20

Every good gift and every perfect gift is from above.

James 1:17

When I left my old lifestyle of Las Vegas entertainment I said, "God, I need to write some gospel songs and make a gospel album. I think I'll call it *Transformed,* for I believe I have been transformed from the inside out by Your Son, Jesus Christ."

I started writing gospel songs, and the first song I wrote was titled "He is the Way, the Truth, and the Life" from John 14:6.

The first time I ever sang it was at Pastor Gary Green-wall's Eagle's Nest Church in Southern California: just me and my accoustic guitar. When I came on the stage, Pastor Gary handed me an offering. It was fifty dollars. I could receive it as a blessing, or I could take it as an insult and

walk out of the church mad. But I went into the bathroom stall, and I got on my knees and thanked God that He was going to take care of me.

The same week I sang at another church, and that morning I said to the Lord, "I thank You for my new album. Send someone to help me." I got there and shared a little of what I know—that Jesus saved me—and I sang my song. After the service a businessman who had been seated on the back row came up and asked me if I would like to record a gospel album. He was the president of Shalom Record Company of Oklahoma City.

He flew me to Oklahoma City and put up probably $20,000, using the best of the best muscians for me. When the album, *Transformed,* came out, it became a top-ten record in the American Gospel Charts. We did another gospel record together titled *Glory,* and it became number two on the gospel charts.

Jesus said, **Give, and it shall be given unto you; good measure, pressed down, and shaken together, and running over, shall men give into your bosom** (Luke 6:38).

That's an incredible truth! The song "He is the Way" has earned over a million dollars, and I have been able to put the money back into the gospel. With the psalmist, I say, "I will sing unto the Lord because he has done bountifully with me." (Ps. 13:6.) Seeing what God can do with what I give Him really makes my life full of excitement and joy.

Trust God, and He will do the same for you.

Our church has had it's challenges. We started out calling it the Harvest Family Church because we knew we were here to show people the Lord of the Harvest and hope for their families. After we got everything printed up, we got a call from a small local church's pastor who was threatening to sue us for using that name because he had it first. We changed the name, of course, to Family Harvest Church, and we started all over. Praise God, we have seen His harvest of families grow.

My mother, Lillie; my step-dad, "Pop" Charlie; and my sister, "Sissy" Athylene, have all moved to Phoenix and are members of Family Harvest Church. They have each been a great help in building God's church here and such a comfort to have near. We have had many special guests, including Norvel Hayes, Betty Jean Robinson, Jeff Fenholt and many others.

God has blessed us.

The Word of God prevails. We bought a $500,000 property and have expanded the existing church twice. Now we have added a brand new sanctuary, and it is debt-free.

We started with a $1000 seed of faith, and God has blessed Family Harvest Church. Today it is worth one million dollars and is debt-free. We give God all the glory.

God is more than enough as we see people come and go. Some God leads, and some lead themselves; but we stay faithful to His call, because every person is important to God.

That's why He cares so much that we turn to Him. The Bible says in John 10:10 that there is a thief who comes "to

steal and to kill and destroy." But Jesus said, "I am come that they might have life, and that they might have it more abundantly."

Yes, the Bible teaches us everything we need to know to live and how to overcome in every area of our lives.

If you call upon the Lord and believe in your heart, He will answer you and save you. (Rom. 10:9.)

John 3:16 says, **For God so loved the world, that he gave his only begotten Son, that whosoever believeth in him should not perish, but have everlasnting life.**

Yes. Faith works, prayer works, love works. I always remember the Scripture from the Bible that I learned from Dad Hagin, and I've always stood on this.

> **Therefore I say unto you, What soever things ye desire, when ye pray believe that ye receive them and ye shall have them.**
>
> **Mark 11:24**

Don't stop believing!

To contact Reggie Vinson,
write:
17803 North 27th Avenue
Phoenix, Arizona 85053-1749

*Please include your prayer requests
and comments when you write.*

THE HARRISON HOUSE VISION

Proclaiming the truth and the power
Of the Gospel of Jesus Christ
With excellence;

Challenging Christians to
Live victoriously,
Grow spiritually,
Know God intimately.